CINCINNATI
HAUNTED HANDBOOK

jeff and
michael morris

clerisy press

Cincinnati Haunted Handbook

COPYRIGHT © 2010 by Jeff Morris and Michael Morris

Published by Clerisy Press
Distributed by Publishers Group West
Printed in the United States of America
First edition, third printing 2016

Library of Congress Cataloging-in-Publication Data
   Morris, Jeff, 1978–
      Cincinnati haunted handbook / by Jeff and Michael Morris.
      p. cm.
      ISBN-13: 978-1-57860-469-2
      ISBN-10: 1-57860-469-9
      1. Haunted places—Ohio—Cincinnati—Guidebooks. 2. Ghosts—Ohio—Cincinnati—Guidebooks. 3. Cincinnati (Ohio)—Guidebooks. I. Morris, Michael A., 1981– II. Title.

      BF1472.U6M678 2010
      133.109771'78--dc22
                      2010020571

Edited by Jack Heffron
Cover photo by Jeff and Michael Morris
Back cover photo by Jeff and Michael Morris
All interior photos by Jeff and Michael Morris
Text design by Annie Long

Clerisy Press
An imprint of AdventureKEEN
306 Greenup Street
Covington, KY 41011
www.clerisypress.com

DEDICATION

For Tina,

While each passing day makes it harder and harder to remember your face,
I will never forgot those things that you taught me,
That helping others when I can,
That always wearing a smile,
Can make anyone, even me, a better person.

While you're gone now,
The world is a better place for what you once were.

Despite our friendship having been brief,
It was a privilege to have known you.

CONTENTS

SECTION I cemeteries

SECTION II roads and bridges

SECTION III parks and trails

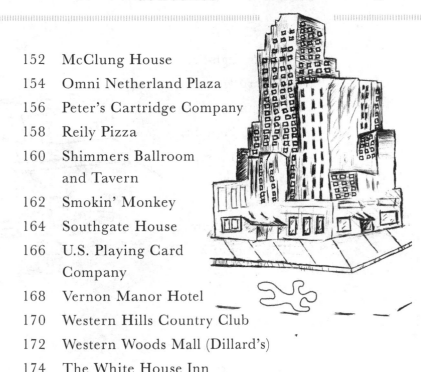

SECTION VI schools and public buildings

ACKNOWLEDGMENTS

So many people out there helped to make this book possible. Since there is such an eclectic and vast number of locations, histories, and ghosts in this book, it was necessary to speak with a large number of people and to use a variety of resources to bring all of this together. I would like to start by thanking all of those people whose names I have forgotten and those people whose names I never had the chance to get. Without these people, this book would not have come to be, and I apologize profusely to those who helped me that I have left out of this section.

This being said, there are many other people who helped me with the book whose names I do have. Some of these people, I simply and fortunately remembered to record their names, and others I have the privilege and honor to call my friends. The following list of people are ghost researchers, business owners, and other people who have lived in this haunted city who have helped me acquire both ghost stories and history from many of these locations. Many of the ghost researchers and investigators from this list were actually kind enough to write blurbs about their own paranormal experiences, and they did not ask for anything in return: Michele Hale, Matt Hoskins, Noah Carlisle, Sarah McEvoy, Helen Ryan, Chris Maggard, Christel Brooks, Melinda Smith, Nick Sakelos, Diane Bachman, Scott Santangelo, Jeff Craig, Joedy Cook, Garett Merk, Lisa Edwards, Tristan Goins, Diane Ward, Jennifer Adams, Sgt. Ron Reckers, Sir Fred.

Beyond these people, there are several organizations that aided immensely in the research necessary for this book: Whitewater Township Historical Society, Delhi Historical Society, Indian Hill Historical Society, Liberty Township Historical Society, Cincinnati Historical Society, Public Libraries of Cincinnati and Hamilton County, Butler County Historical Society, Mt. Healthy Historical Society, the Knights of the Golden Trail, Cincinnati Paranormal, Cincinnati Regional Association for Paranormal Studies, Southern Ohio Apparition Researchers, Northern Kentucky Paranormal Society, Tri State Paranormal of Northern Kentucky, Paranormal Researchers of Northern Kentucky, Tristate Paranormal and Oddities Observation Practitioners.

Further, there are several people who I would like to mention individually for the contributions they made to this book.

I would like to thank Rick Fenbers and Ray Lykins for their contributions to the chapter on Satan's Hollow. When I was working on my first book with my brother, we spent countless hours researching the city of Blue Ash, looking for any clue to the location of this old tunnel system. We found nothing and had all but given up the search when we learned from Rick and Ray that they had finally found it. It is due to the adventurous nature of Rick and Ray from Cincinnati Regional Association for Paranormal Studies that this chapter has made its way into this book. They should be considered an inspiration to all of those potential paranormal explorers in this city and around the world.

Next, I would like to thank Joy Naylor. Not only is Joy a close friend of mine, but she is responsible for many of the ghost stories in the book, especially those stories from the Indian Hill and Norwood areas of town. I approached her one day asking for any ghost stories she knew from the city, and she began listing them off faster than I could write them down. It is entirely due to her that many of the stories from Indian Hill, Hyde Park, Norwood, and Milford wound up in this book. She was always anxious to help all she could, and she deserves my sincere gratitude.

Next, I would like to thank Jack Heffron, my publisher. Without him, this book would still likely be little more than notes and ideas. When I pitched the idea for the book to him, he was immediately excited about it and has championed it throughout its development. Jack has helped carry this book from its inception to where it is today and more importantly has fought for it, unwilling to let the idea die at any stage. In more ways than one, this is his book.

Finally, I would like to thank my friends and family who helped keep me sane throughout the countless hours of work that went into this book, especially my wife, Amy, who picked up my slack at home while I was out photographing, researching, and writing.

INTRODUCTION

MY TWO GREATEST INTERESTS ARE, first, the paranormal and, second, history. The reason I have placed these two fields of study in this order is because, essentially, this is the order that they became my top interests. In 2005, I lived near a road in Cincinnati that was reputed to be haunted. I cannot explain in great detail why this rumor excited me so much beyond the fact that it seemed to be something completely unexplored in my own mind. For me, ghosts were the stuff of horror movies and television shows. When I heard that there was supposedly some real paranormal entity within walking distance from my house, I was very excited. I probably drove down that road hundreds of times hoping to experience something paranormal. Though I never did, I kept going back again and again. It did not matter that I had not seen anything. Other people had, so the possibility was there that I could.

Through my interest in this road, I began to learn that there were many haunted places all over the city. My brother Mike and I would take little paranormal road trips at night, visiting these haunted locations in hopes of somehow running into a ghost. As we began to explore these places, we became more and more interested in the ghost stories themselves. The stories were great, and the possibility that there was really a ghost at these places was exciting, but we decided to look further into the stories themselves. We wanted to see if there was any truth in them—not so much in the ghosts but in the history of what happened at these locations and the reasons that, perhaps, ghosts lurked there among the living. This is where my interest in history was born. As my brother and I started to uncover the history of these haunted locations, the history of the city itself came to life for us. Therefore, I guess I owe thanks to the ghosts of Cincinnati for teaching me so much about this city's history.

The ghost stories and the histories of these locations make up a major part of this book, which I feel they definitely should. The ghost stories are more interesting with a historical background, and the reason that any of these locations are in this book is that they are haunted. That being said, this book also contains a couple of other facets that I have not really seen in other ghost books. The locations, histories, and ghost stories are quite interesting in themselves, but this book also offers the opportunity to visit these locations. Each chapter includes detailed directions on how to get to these places and descriptions of how to visit them. All the directions begin from downtown Cincinnati to give you a common place to start your road trips.

When my brother and I were looking for these haunted locations, we would have been thrilled to have a manual to explain how to find them. I cannot even estimate the number of hours we spent looking fruitlessly for a location. For those readers who are not great at following directions but who have a GPS unit, we have also included the addresses, which you can plug into your GPS.

The other section in each chapter details how to visit these haunted locations. Mike and I certainly could have used that information during our moonlight searches. We had to learn the hard way which locations closed after dark and which ones the police frequented at night, hoping to catch cars stopping in the middle of the road flashing their lights. This section in each chapter tells you the best way to visit these locations and gives you what we feel is the best chance of actually encountering a spirit.

Perhaps my favorite aspect of this book is the daunting number of locations included in it—and all of them just a short drive away. In the past, I've found myself flipping through many other ghost books looking for stories of nearby locations. I would end up reading only a couple of stories, ones focused on places I knew.

In the *Haunted Handbook* you'll find one hundred locations within the Greater Cincinnati area, which is large enough to offer quite a number of stories but small enough that local people have some sense of where to go. We did our best to ensure that no two locations in the book were more than an hour apart. We've found at least one place in nearly every area of the city.

We feel that this book is the quintessential guide for hunting ghosts in the Greater Cincinnati area—as well as an entertaining and informative guide for those hunters who don't want to leave their chairs. We hope you find it interesting, and we hope future ghosthunters learn about the history and the ghosts here in this great city.

Enjoy.

IMPORTANT *Read this before you start the book!*

Before we begin, and before you begin your ghostly adventures around Cincinnati, it is imperative that you understand the following three points.

Keep your own safety in mind at all times.

Many of these locations can be dangerous to visit, especially at night and especially if you're not constantly careful and aware of your surroundings. Many of the ghost stories take place on remote roads where you are required to stop your car to see the resident spirits. If you decide to stop and wait, make sure you are aware of other cars on the road. You have to make sure that if a car is approaching, you are able to get out of the way.

Also, there are several locations that are not in the safest neighborhoods of the city. While you are in these areas, make sure you're safe. Don't make yourself and whatever expensive equipment you bring targets for someone out in the middle of the night with somewhat darker intentions than yourself.

Cincinnati already has enough ghosts. We don't want you to create another one.

Obey the law.

Unfortunately, some of the paranormal phenomena in this book occurs at night in places that close after dark. Do not trespass in these places! Look for signs that state visiting hours, and if they are closed do not enter them without permission. The possibility of seeing a ghost is not worth the probability of getting arrested or fined for trespassing.

This book is not meant to encourage you to break the law. If we state that something is illegal, simply do not do it. You will suffer the consequences and will encourage tougher regulations at these places to prevent people from breaking the law in the future.

Show respect.

While all of the locations in this book are reputed to have some sort of ghostly activity, all of the locations also serve another purpose. Cemeteries are places of memories and reverence. If you are yelling and screaming when you enter a cemetery, this is an unforgivable sign of disrespect to both those who are buried there and to those whose friends and family are buried there. Some of the roads in this book are near houses. If you are playing around on these roads in the middle of the night, you could wake up people in the neighborhood. These people are sure to call the police, and the police are sure to keep closer watch on these areas and ruin these ghost stories for the rest of us.

There are also businesses in this book. While these businesses are reputed to be haunted, the ghosts are not their main source of revenue. These businesses have to continue to operate even with their ghosts, so if you enter these places looking for ghosts, make sure that you are not disrupting the regular flow of business.

As the author of this book, I cannot take responsibility for those who choose to disregard these warnings. This book is meant to encourage people to learn about and even experience the ghosts and history of Cincinnati, not to in any way hurt anyone or to upset the community. Keep your adventures legal, keep them respectful, and above all keep them safe.

HAPPY GHOSTING!

Gravestone carving at Spring Grove Cemetery and Arboretum, see profile on pages 30-31.

SECTION I

cemeteries

Cemeteries are often haunted, as if the dead have a hard time leaving their physical bodies behind. Much of their world seems to consist of wandering aimlessly through cemeteries or repeating trivial gestures that they often did in life. While many of these actions may seem meaningless, we need to make sure that when the dead do have something important to say…

we're listening.

ADATH ISRAEL CEMETERY

1661 Sunset Avenue, Cincinnati, OH 45238

directions

Take I-75 to the Harrison Avenue exit. Follow the signs that direct you to Queen City Avenue. Follow Queen City Avenue a little more than a mile up the hill and turn left onto Sunset Avenue. Follow Sunset for less than a mile. Adath Israel will be on your left just after you pass the intersection with Guerley Road.

history

When the cholera epidemic hit Cincinnati in the 1840s, the only Jewish cemetery in the city filled up quickly. As a result, many Jewish communities throughout the area created more cemeteries. Adath Israel Cemetery in Price Hill was one of them.

This cemetery eventually was filled to capacity, and the congregation of the temple started another one elsewhere in the city and discontinued burials at the Price Hill location, but this is the one that is reputed to be haunted.

In 2008, a group vandalized several headstones, and the cemetery now is watched more closely by law enforcement and by concerned neighbors at night.

ghost story

Most of the ghost stories from this cemetery take place in the caretaker's building. This red-brick building sits within the cemetery itself. The paranormal events tend to occur in the basement. A chair will move around all by itself. Lights in the basement will come on by themselves. Other times voices and figures will be seen and heard throughout the basement despite the fact that the building is empty. When curious onlookers gaze through the windows into the basement, sometimes they will see strange reflections of figures standing behind them. When these terrified witnesses turn around, no one is there.

The caretaker's building, however, isn't the only haunted location in this cemetery. People will often see figures walking among the headstones, especially at night. When people approach the area where they saw these figures, no one is found.

visiting

It's probably best to visit this cemetery during the day, when it is easier to look through the basement windows in the caretaker's house and see how the basement is set up. Most of the stories involve things that happen during the day because that is when people are usually around. I have caught interesting EVPs at the cemetery during the day.

Recently, the caretakers and owners of the cemetery have posted warnings that the cemetery closes at nine p.m., meaning that it is illegal to enter the cemetery at night. Unfortunately, this limitation probably resulted from the vandals who uprooted several headstones—an example of how one group of insensitive people can end up ruining a place for the rest of us.

BETH ISRAEL CEMETERY

Pleasant Avenue and Hill Avenue, Fairfield, OH 45014

directions

Take I-75 North to I-275 West. From I-275 take the Hamilton Ave/SR-127 exit (exit 36) and turn right on Hamilton Ave/SR-127. Hamilton Avenue changes its name to Pleasant Avenue. Follow this road for about five miles until you cross Hill Avenue. Just past Hill Avenue on Pleasant, Beth Israel Cemetery will be on your left. There is a Catholic cemetery across the street on your right.

history

This cemetery was built in response to the need for more Jewish cemeteries throughout the Cincinnati area. In 1849 when the cholera epidemic hit Cincinnati, there was just one Jewish cemetery in the city. Cholera quickly filled this cemetery so the Jewish community built several others in the Greater Cincinnati area to fulfill the need for consecrated Jewish burial grounds. Today it is still in operation, and it is well kept.

ghost story

This cemetery is supposedly a hotbed for EVP activity. I have not run across any stories of figures or even ghostly, disembodied sounds coming at any time of the day or night, but I have heard about people recording a strange voice they didn't hear at the time they were there. Many times the recordings feature human whispers, but some include a barking dog or a ringing church bell that wasn't heard when the recording was made.

visiting

As far as I can tell, this cemetery is open throughout the night. There are no signs on the gates advertising any hours of operation, and the gates are always open. I have come to this cemetery many times during the late hours of the night and have never been approached or questioned as to my intentions there.

At the same time, I can't stress enough how important it is that you stay respectful within the cemetery, especially if you are there late at night. If people are running around, yelling, and screaming, someone is sure to call the police, and although it doesn't close at night, I would be on the side of any police officer who arrests someone being disrespectful in a cemetery. If you go there late at night, quietly make a recording and ask respectful questions to those who are there—those who seem so anxious to speak with the living.

CONGRESS GREEN CEMETERY
50 Cliff Road, North Bend, OH 45052

directions
From Cincinnati, take Route 50 west all the way to North Bend or take I-74 West to the SR 128 exit (exit 7) and follow 128 south until you reach Route 50. Turn left on Route 50. Turn onto Miami Avenue in North Bend. There should be a sign pointing you to the tomb of William Henry Harrison. Follow Miami Avenue to Brower Road and turn left on Brower. Turn right onto Cliff Road just after the bridge. Follow the road up the hill past the William Henry Harrison tomb. Parking is on your right; the cemetery is on your left near the top of the hill.

history
The cemetery was built by the man who founded North Bend (not to mention most of the rest of the Cincinnati area). His name was John Cleves Symmes, and he hoped that North Bend would become the jewel of southwest Ohio. In 1814, Symmes was one of the first to be buried in the graveyard. At the time, it was called the Pasture Graveyard. Symmes' son-in-law was President William Henry Harrison, and his great-grandson was President Benjamin Harrison.

In 1878, a man named John Scott Harrison died. He was the son of William Henry Harrison and the father of Benjamin Harrison. He was taken to Congress Green Cemetery, where his children noticed that a grave had been disturbed and the body stolen. To prevent their father's body from being stolen in the same way, they buried him in a concrete vault without a marker. After the funeral, Benjamin Harrison went back to his home in Indiana, but John's other son, John Jr., went looking for the body snatchers. His investigation led him to the Cincinnati Medical College in downtown Cincinnati. As he entered the school to question them about the recent robbery, he found the body of his father, John Scott Harrison, sprawled on a table about to be dissected.

ghost story

People say that John Scott Harrison and John Cleves Symmes both haunt this cemetery. John Scott Harrison supposedly haunts it because of the grave robbery, and John Cleves Symmes haunts it because he is upset that North Bend didn't become the jewel of southwest Ohio. People will hear voices and see figures walking through the cemetery. Sometimes strange mists will rise from certain headstones. Other times people will see men dressed in Civil War uniforms walking through the cemetery.

visiting

The best time to visit this cemetery is during the day. Many ghost hunts have been conducted here during the day, and some strange images have been caught in photographs. The area is kind of out of the way, so many times you will be the only person wandering through the cemetery.

There are clear indications that the cemetery closes at dusk, so it is in your best interest to follow these warnings and leave when the sun goes down. There is a house adjacent to the cemetery, and the owners are likely to report trespassers after dark. Since there has been ghostly activity caught here during the day, it is not worth the risk to break the law and wander into the cemetery at night.

DARBY LEE HISTORIC CEMETERY

5999 Bender Road, Cincinnati, OH 45233

directions

This location is somewhat difficult to find. It is hidden quite well just outside of Delhi. The easiest way to get to this cemetery is to take SR-50 west from Cincinnati toward Delhi. Take a right onto Bender Road up the hill. Near the top of the hill is a retirement community known as Riverview Community. The easiest way to get to the cemetery is to park in the lot of the retirement community. Near the back of the lot, you'll see a rusted metal sign hanging on an old shed directing you into the woods to the Darby Lee Historic Cemetery. Follow the path into the woods for about a hundred feet, and the small overgrown cemetery will be on your left.

history

The story behind this cemetery is quite inspiring. It was an important place along the Underground Railroad in the Cincinnati area. Since Kentucky was a slave state and Ohio a free state, the Ohio River was both a symbolic and physical barrier between slavery and freedom. Crossing the Ohio River was a major step on the slave's escape to freedom, but often it still wasn't safe for escaped slaves in Ohio. There were harsh penalties for anyone known to be harboring a fugitive slave, and the slave would be shipped backed to his or her former owner and would likely be punished severely.

It was therefore imperative that those operating the Underground Railroad work out a system letting the escaped slaves know when it was safe to travel. A man who lived near the location where the Darby Lee Cemetery is today would light a green lantern and play his fiddle when it was safe to cross the river. The fugitive slaves would see the green light on the other side of the river and hear the fiddle music and know when it was safe to cross. Today, the area where the fiddler would guide slaves to freedom is a cemetery. The fiddler was the first person buried at the site.

ghost story

People who have visited this cemetery at night report seeing strange green lights floating around the property. These green lights will either appear to be a green lantern sitting in the forest or will appear as a green glowing ball that floats through the cemetery. The lights always fade away before the witnesses can determine what they are. Other times, people will hear the sound of a fiddle playing in the darkness without any discernible source.

visiting

Several obstacles stand in the way of visiting this remarkable little cemetery. First of all, the closest available parking is within the property of the Riverview Community. While this is the easiest way to get to the cemetery, the property's managers can ask you to move your car if you park there with the sole purpose of going back to the cemetery. They have always been incredibly accommodating to me and have never asked me to leave, but I have always visited the site during the day and have always kept a polite silence while I was at this cemetery so close to the retirement community.

If you are uncomfortable leaving your car in the lot of the retirement community, there are a couple of other options that are available to you. You can find a place to park down on River Road/SR-50. There is a building at the corner of River Road and Bender that if you walk up to the end of their parking lot, there is a trail that goes off into the woods. Your car will be towed if you park in that lot, but you can use the lot to walk up to this trail. Simply follow the long trail up into the woods. The cemetery will be on the right.

There is another trail up near the Mt Saint Joseph Motherhouse on the other end of Bender Road. If you park up near Mt. Saint Joseph College (you cannot park in the Motherhouse lot), you can walk past the Motherhouse cemetery to another trail that moves off into the woods. If you follow this trail, it will take you past the retirement community and to the cemetery.

While there is nothing suggesting that this cemetery closes after dark, there is another obstacle that stands in a visitor's way after dark. This obstacle is that it is very hard to navigate the trail after dark. The woods are very thick in this area, and the trail is very skinny and difficult to find at times even in the daylight. You need to make sure that you have a strong flashlight and a strong sense of direction when traveling into these woods at night. My suggestion to you is that you find your way to the cemetery near dusk so that there is still some daylight by which to navigate the trail. That way you can experience the cemetery at night and possibly see those mysterious green lights. After you have finished your investigation, the easiest way out would probably be the nearby retirement community parking lot. Then follow Bender Road to wherever you had parked your car.

HOPEWELL CEMETERY

6471 Camden College Corner Road, College Corner, OH 45003

directions

Take I-75 north to I-275 west. Take I-275 to the Colerain Avenue exit, and take Colerain Avenue/US-27 north toward Butler County. Continue to follow US-27, turning left when you get into Millville onto Millville Oxford Road. Follow this road all the way into Oxford and then turn left onto East High Street. Then turn right onto North Main Street/OH-732. Continue to follow OH-732, turning left after five miles onto Hamilton Richmond Road. Follow Hamilton Richmond Road/OH-732 for another three miles then turn left onto Camden College Corner Road. The cemetery and church will be on your right.

history

This cemetery was the first public cemetery in Israel Township and is one of the oldest cemeteries in all of Preble County. The first burial here was in 1813. A man named Thomas McDill returned home from the War of 1812 with an illness that soon took his life. Many Revolutionary War veterans and Civil War Veterans have been buried here throughout the years. More than a thousand graves populate this small graveyard.

Perhaps the strangest and most tragic thing about this cemetery is the number of children who are buried here. Most of the graves hold children under the age of eighteen. Much of this is due to several epidemics that swept through the area in the 1840s—primarily cholera as well as other diseases. Hopewell became almost a monument to all those children who were lost throughout the years.

ghost story

This creepy cemetery in the middle of nowhere is reputed to be one of the most haunted cemeteries in the southwestern part of Ohio. Through the years many strange stories have been told about this graveyard.

Some of the more common and harmless ghost stories involve strange lights. People who visit at night will sometimes see what appears to be a light from a lantern bouncing along throughout the cemetery. Other reports simply involve a floating ball of light that weaves its way through the headstones. On one side of the church, which stands in the middle of the graveyard, there is a motion-sensor light that will come on if anyone is near the entrance. People report that this light will often turn on by itself, even when there is no one close to the church.

Another somewhat harmless phenomenon involves voices that seem to come from all around the cemetery. These voices are so clear that the witnesses are certain there is someone else nearby. The strange thing, though, is that this place is so isolated there is almost no feasible way that someone could be way out in the middle of nowhere without a car. If anyone drove up, the car would be easy to see in the surrounding area.

Other stories about the cemetery are not quite so harmless. According to legend, if you visit this place at night, you will be plagued by bad luck. Another story says that if you leave your car and walk through the cemetery, when you return to your car there will be a surprise waiting for you inside. Unfortunately, anyone who has received this surprise refuses to reveal what it is, saying only that it startled them so much when they saw it that they almost ran their car off the road.

visiting

Hopewell Cemetery closes at dusk. This time limit is clearly posted on a sign just inside the cemetery. Since most of the paranormal activity only takes place at night, the closing time is unfortunate for us ghost hunters.

The cemetery is quite isolated. There are very few houses anywhere near this place. The graveyard is on the outskirts of Hueston Woods State Park, a large expanse of wilderness in itself. You can still see the stars from out here. This isolation adds to the creepiness of the place and makes it easy to see if there are other people in the area. It would be difficult to get to this place without a car, and your car would be clearly visible from the road.

It is completely legal to stand outside the walls of the cemetery and look into it. This is your best bet if you want to see the ghosts without trespassing. The lights should be visible from the road and the voices should be clearly audible. You can even just sit in your car on the road and listen. It is rare that another car will go down the road late at night, and if another car is coming, you can pull away or pull over and let the other car pass.

KINGS ISLAND CEMETERY

6300 Kings Island Drive, Mason, OH 45040

directions

Take I-71 North from Cincinnati to exit 24, Western Row Road. At the end of the exit, go straight at the traffic light. Kings Island will be on your right. The cemetery is just off the road to your right. The cemetery is between the Kings Island parking lot and the Great Wolf Lodge parking lot on Kings Island Drive. It is easy to miss so keep careful watch for it just past the last exit from the Kings Island lot onto Kings Island Drive.

history

Before Kings Island dominated the landscape in this area, a small nondescript cemetery sat along the road surrounded by a picket fence. Some of the headstones in the cemetery date back to the mid 1800s, and some of the words on the headstones have faded to the point where they are illegible.

Today the cemetery seems like an anachronism surrounded by modern wonders. On one side of the cemetery is the main road. On another side stands the Great Wolf Lodge, a large indoor water park and hotel. And on the remaining two sides are Kings Island Amusement Park and the parking lot. This small cemetery seems dominated and almost forgotten amid all of this development. Perhaps it is this domination that has encouraged ghosts to come out. Perhaps the ghosts just don't want to be forgotten.

ghost story

The most famous ghost from this small cemetery is a young girl. She is often seen in Kings Island itself in the area between the water park and the amusement park, but she is also seen in the cemetery. People will see her standing inside the wooden fence, looking out toward the amusement park. Many times when people see her, they only see her out of the corner of their eyes on the way out of the parking lot. By the time they realize that it's too late at night for a girl as young as she to be inside the little cemetery, they have past her.

Other people will feel unwelcoming presences when they are inside the cemetery, or they will feel like they are being watched. At night, people will often see shadowy figures moving throughout the cemetery, especially when they are driving out of the park through the exit near the cemetery.

visiting

The biggest obstacle to visiting this cemetery during the day is parking. It costs money to park in Kings Island's lot, and there is really no parking anywhere else near the small cemetery. It seems the only options are to park down the street at the theater or pay for parking at the amusement park.

Once you are parked, you still might face some obstacles. Although there are no signs that say anything about the cemetery closing at dark, it is possible that the cemetery is off limits at that time. Kings Island is heavily guarded after closing, so it is likely that you will be approached by security if you are in the cemetery after hours.

If you are visiting the park itself, the cemetery might be a stop to consider on your way out or in. I personally wouldn't suggest you go to the cemetery in the middle of the night when Kings Island is closed. I went once in the middle of the day during the off-season when Kings Island was closed for the winter. I was not approached by anyone while I was there.

MIAMITOWN CEMETERY

Corner of Mill Street and State Route 128, Cleves, OH 45041

directions

Take I-74 to exit 7 (SR-128 Cleves/Hamilton). Take SR-128 north toward Wendy's and BP. The cemetery will be on your left. Just past the cemetery, turn left on Mill Street. There is diagonal parking alongside the cemetery.

history

The current cemetery is a conglomeration of several other cemeteries that have been combined. On the north side of Miamitown, there is a street called Cemetery Road near the Village Pump antique store. There was once a cemetery here, but it was moved. The headstones were moved across town to the new cemetery, but when workers attempted to move the bodies, the old wooden caskets broke apart, and they decided that moving the bodies would be too difficult. The headstones remain at the current cemetery but the bodies have been paved over and are still underground at Cemetery Road.

Another cemetery, which was located where the elementary school sits today, was moved across the street to the churchyard (see Miamitown Elementary chapter in the Schools and Public Buildings section of this book). This time both the bodies and the headstones were moved. Unfortunately, there were many unmarked graves in the original cemetery so when they dug up the ground to build the school, they dug up piles of bodies. They had no idea who these people were, so they simply reburied the bodies across the street at the current cemetery without markers.

Further, a caretaker who once worked at the current cemetery didn't like broken headstones in his cemetery, so whenever a headstone broke, he would tear it out of the ground and throw it into the Great Miami River. The section of the graveyard that is today the municipal cemetery, the area closest to the old Methodist Church, is completely full despite the fact that there are hardly any headstones in the area.

ghost story

Various paranormal phenomena occurs at the cemetery. People will feel very uncomfortable while they are here, especially at night. They either will feel as if they are being watched, or they will feel chills crawling up and down their spines. Other times, people will actually feel an icy finger touch them on the back of their necks. Shadowy figures will also roam throughout the cemetery and then vanish.

The most famous ghost of the cemetery, however, is a little girl in a white dress. When people see the little girl, she will often vanish immediately or linger until the witness approaches her.

visiting

This cemetery is open throughout the night, so you do not need to worry about legal issues after dark. The haunted area is the section between the Methodist Church and the blacktop road that wraps around the church in the shape of an 'L'. The remainder of the cemetery is private—known as the Miami Cemetery—and officially closes after dark. If you stay on the church side of the road, you are free to search for ghosts throughout the night. Just make sure you are respectful while inside the cemetery gates.

MILLVILLE CEMETERY

2289 Millville Avenue, Hamilton, OH 45013

directions

Take I-75 north to I-275 west. Take I-275 to the Colerain Avenue exit. Take Colerain Avenue/US-27 north past Ross until the road seems to dead end in Millville. At this point there is a sign saying that Oxford is to your left and Hamilton is to your right. To the left is Millville Oxford Road and to the right is Millville Avenue. Turn right onto Millville Avenue and follow this road for a couple miles. Millville Cemetery will be on your right. There will be a bright blue sign near the road.

history

Millville Cemetery is much older than it appears. Most of the headstones look relatively new, but this cemetery dates all the way back to 1822. Its newer appearance is probably due, at least in part, to the fact that it is now the only active cemetery in the immediate Hanover Township/Millville area. The cemetery averages more than sixty burials a year so many of the headstones are new. Many of the original headstones from the early to mid 1800s are lost among the newer ones.

In 2005, the Board of Trustees of Hanover Township purchased more land to expand the cemetery, which should be able to add new graves until at least 2045.

ghost story

Millville Cemetery seems to be a hotbed of paranormal activity. Perhaps this activity is due to the clash between the spirits of the older graves and the new burials that happen every year. Perhaps the older spirits are concerned that they will be forgotten, so they make themselves known.

People will often see full apparitions in the cemetery. While the encounters most often happen at night, they have been known to happen at dawn or dusk or during cloudy or rainy days. Two apparitions are seen most often. The first one is an old man that people will see walking aimlessly around the cemetery. The old man will roam around for a while, seemingly looking for something and then will vanish. The second apparition is that of a young girl, who is seen standing near one of the trees near the front of the cemetery. She always stares out toward the field to the west of the cemetery.

Visitors also talk of seeing strange balls of light that seem to float through the cemetery, and of feeling cold spots on warm days.

visiting

Unfortunately, this cemetery closes at night, which means you cannot explore during the time when most of the activity is reported to occur. But you can see into the cemetery from the road at night. If you park your car up the street and walk down to the area just outside the gates of the cemetery, you can look in without trespassing. The apparitions of the man and the young girl are often seen within view of the main road.

Also, you might try exploring on rainy or cloudy days. The ghosts are sometimes seen when the sun isn't shining. The cemetery is open until dusk, and people have experienced paranormal activity just before closing.

PRICE HILL POTTER'S FIELD

4700 Guerley Road, Cincinnati, OH 45238

directions

Take I-75 to the Harrison Avenue exit. At the exit, follow the signs to Queen City Avenue. Follow Queen City up the hill for a couple miles and then turn left at the traffic light onto Sunset Avenue. Follow Sunset until you get to Guerley Road and then turn right onto Guerley. A half-mile up the road, at the first private driveway on your right, is a sign for the potter's field. The actual graveyard is in the thick woods just to the right of the sign. The section of the potter's field directly adjacent to the private driveway is protected by a barbed wire fence. Walk past the driveway to a dirt access road, and follow the access road. Turn into the woods on your right when you see anything that may pass for a path. This is the potter's field. It is completely overgrown. Since you cannot park in the private drive, you may have to park at the CVS pharmacy a quarter mile farther down Guerley and then walk down to the cemetery.

history

When the cholera epidemic struck Cincinnati in 1849, there was a desperate need for cemeteries throughout the city. Many were created based on the religious faith of those buried there, but there was also the need for potter's fields—cemeteries built on non-consecrated ground for those too poor or too 'evil' to be buried in faith-specific graveyards. The potter's field in Price Hill was built in 1849.

During its years of operation, an estimated 6,000 to 10,000 people were buried in the graveyard. Many were buried without markers, and many markers used during the operation of the graveyard have been lost through the years. During the time when a tuberculosis hospital was located at Dunham, the patients and staff participated in the upkeep of the cemetery. Some of the patients were buried in this cemetery since few people wanted to bury tubercular patients for fear of getting the disease themselves. By the time the cemetery closed down, upkeep had become a problem. In 1981, the city of Cincinnati decided not to continue upkeep of the cemetery, which quickly became completely overgrown.

ghost story

This cemetery is quite haunted. People will hear strange voices and sobbing coming from the grounds at night. When people walk through during the day or night, they feel that they are being followed or watched. Sometimes people will actually see ghostly figures, which vanish when they are approached.

Perhaps the spirits of all those unfortunate souls who are buried here are upset about the shabby condition of the cemetery or about having been buried in a potter's field. The ghosts here always seem to give off an angry and menacing vibe.

visiting

A couple of obstacles stand in the way of visiting this cemetery: parking and access. It is difficult to find a place to park. The sign for the cemetery is situated beside a driveway on Guerley Road. From what I could ascertain, this is a private driveway, so you cannot park there without permission from the homeowners. Another option is the CVS pharmacy about a quarter mile down the road near the intersection with Glenway. You can park there and walk down to the cemetery. Also, you can park at Dunham Park and head through the woods toward the potter's field. But Dunham closes at ten p.m., and it's easy to get lost in the woods because there is no clear path to the cemetery.

Access to the cemetery is also a problem, though the field is open to the public, and you can enter it legally at any time. In fact, it's  unlikely that anyone would know you're there, even if you had flashlights in the middle of the night. But the area is overgrown and nearly impossible to navigate. There were times during my visit when I literally had to crawl from place to place. For that reason, I suggest visiting during the day. Finding your way around at night through the thick brush is more of a challenge than any ghosthunter should have to face.

There are only a few headstones in the potter's field, but there are some markers. Many of them lay flat along the ground and do not feature names—only numbers. There is at least one stone made of granite with the name and dates carved into it. When visiting the cemetery, try to find these headstones and markers because this is where most of the activity is rumored to occur.

REILY CEMETERIES

Reily Cemetery—Peoria Reily Road, Reily, OH 45056

Springdale Cemetery—Springdale Road, Reily, OH 45056

Indian Creek Church Burial Ground—N 39 degrees 27' 52.3"
  W 84 degrees 47' 11.4"

Pioneer Cemetery—N 39 degrees 25' 13.3" W 84 degrees 43' 56.9"

directions

Take I-75 north to I-275 west. Take I-275 to the Colerain Avenue/US-27 exit and take US-27 north. Follow this road for about ten and a half miles past Ross until you are almost to the traffic light in Millville. Turn left onto OH-129/High Street. Follow OH-129 for about six miles and then turn right onto Sample Road/OH-732. Follow this road for about three miles to take you into Reily.

The cemeteries are scattered throughout the area. When you get into Reily, if you turn left onto Main Street, you will find the largest two cemeteries in the area. At the fork in Main Street, if you go left, Reily Cemetery will be on your left; if you go right at the fork, Springdale Cemetery will be on your right. The other cemeteries are tougher to find because they are overgrown and now are hidden in the woods near the town.

history

According to some rumors and legends, in 1807, when the cemeteries of Reily were being built and their locations plotted, those responsible decided to arrange them according to their own religious beliefs—which were quite unusual for the time. These rumors state that the people involved were part of either a pagan or a satanic cult and set up these cemeteries in the shape of a pentagram for religious purposes. (See Reily Pizza chapter in the Businesses section of this book.)

The first thing you may notice when approaching the cemeteries in Reily is that there are a lot of them in a small area with a sparse population. At least four cemeteries are situated within a couple miles of the town's limits: Reily Cemetery, Springdale Cemetery, Indian Creek Church Burial Ground, and Pioneer Cemetery.

Since there are only four cemeteries, the pentagram theory seems unlikely, at first, but there were at least two other cemeteries that have been removed to make room for farmland. While the setup of the known historic cemeteries and those that still exist do not make up a perfect pentagram, there are many ways to connect these cemeteries into a slightly flawed pentagram.

Through the years, these cemeteries have hosted several satanic rituals, and there have been rumors of rituals of witchcraft being performed in the woods near these cemeteries.

ghost story

Every cemetery in the Reily area is reputed to be haunted. Many people claim they simply feel uncomfortable when entering any of them. They say that they feel as if the entire area has been overtaken by a thick atmosphere of evil. People feel they are being watched or that there is a constant evil presence alongside them. This feeling occurs during the day but often is more pronounced at night.

People will also hear chanting from the woods nearby. Those who hear the chanting are never sure if these are ghostly remnants of the dark rituals that are rumored to have gone on or if rituals still go on here.

The spot that is reputed to be the most evil is within Reily Cemetery—a stone monument that is shaped like an angel. For some reason, the arms of the angel have been removed. People feel most uncomfortable near this angel and some suggest that the statue is possessed by some sort of demonic entity.

visiting

It is a terrible idea to enter any Reily Cemetery at night. First of all, the cemeteries all close at night, and this is clearly posted on signs. Local sheriffs know the rumors that these places are haunted, and they know that thrill seekers will attempt to enter the cemeteries after closing time. If you try to get in, you will probably be caught. The Indian Creek Church Burial Ground actually has two gates that you need to pass through to access the cemetery, each posted with warnings that they will prosecute to the fullest extent of the law if you pass these gates.

Many of these cemeteries are actually visible from the road, so while you may not get the full effect of ghosthunting them, you may see some strange things. And many people get the same dark feelings during the day as well. The town of Reily is creepy enough after dark; you don't need to break the law and enter the cemeteries to truly experience the hauntings here.

ROSE HILL CEMETERY

171 South Mason Montgomery Road, Mason, OH 45040

directions

Take I-71 north to the Fields Ertel exit. Turn left onto Mason Montgomery Road. Travel about four and a half miles down the road until you see Rose Hill Cemetery on your left. Once you enter through the main gate, go to your right toward the office. Drive past the office and slightly to your left. The McClung family plot is marked by a large family obelisk covered with names. Rebecca and John's headstones face the street.

history

John McClung was a very jealous person who would rarely, if ever, let his wife Rebecca out of the house. One day in 1901, a scream was heard from the McClung house. When neighbors rushed to see what had happened, Rebecca lay dead in the bedroom, and John was covered with her blood. She had been beaten to death with a log from the fireplace. Her body was moved to the basement of the house while her plot was prepared, and then she was moved a short distance down the road to Rose Hill Cemetery and the family plot.

John was put on trial for murder. He claimed that he was outside at the barn, but everyone knew that he had killed her. The trial drew headlines, and John was demonized in the media for the brutal murder. Somehow though, he was acquitted of the crime. Further, in 1904, he was buried in the plot directly beside Rebecca, the woman he was accused of brutally murdering. (see McClung House chapter in the Businesses section of this book)

ghost story

Rebecca is seen in the cemetery at night. She is most often seen walking up to her own headstone. She appears to be a real person. She is not misty or a momentary shadow. She appears as a full apparition that looks exactly as Rebecca looked in life. Witnesses will be shown a picture of Rebecca and will swear that it was the same person. When she is approached, she always vanishes suddenly. People suggest that she roams the cemetery at night because she is upset that her murderer and oppressor is buried in the plot directly beside her and that he got away with her murder.

visiting

The McClung plot is very difficult to see from the road at night, and unfortunately, the cemetery closes at dark. This makes it difficult to witness the ghost here since she appears mostly at dark or at dusk. Most of the time, this ghost is spotted at night by caretakers who think there is a woman trespassing after closing time.

Your best bet for legally spotting this ghost is to go to the cemetery and wait near the McClung headstone until dusk. Sometimes she is spotted while the cemetery is still open, but you will probably want to leave as soon as it gets dark so that you are not arrested for trespassing.

SPRING GROVE CEMETERY AND ARBORETUM

4521 Spring Grove Avenue, Cincinnati, OH 45232

directions

From downtown Cincinnati, take I-75 North to I-74. Take exit 19 off I-74, the Elmore Street/Spring Grove Avenue exit. At the end of the exit, turn right onto Colerain Avenue. Colerain will dead end into Spring Grove Avenue. Turn left onto Spring Grove Avenue. Follow this road for a little longer than two miles. Spring Grove Cemetery and Arboretum will be on the left. A large gothic gate marks the entrance.

history

Spring Grove is the second-largest cemetery in the country, covering a total of 733 acres. The cemetery was officially chartered in 1845 as the population of Cincinnati began to grow quickly, and many of the existing cemeteries were filling up. The need became even greater in the late 1840s when a cholera epidemic struck the city. Over the years, the cemetery has grown and many of the city's most important names are buried here.

The cemetery also contains the remains of those involved in some tragic occurrences and unusual demises. A famous Negro League baseball player who was killed by a runaway car while sitting on the front stoop of an apartment building is buried here as well as a judge who was killed in the Mount Auburn incline disaster in 1889. The man whose death sparked the deadly Courthouse Riots in Cincinnati in 1884 is also buried here.

Spring Grove was created by a landscape architect to look like a park. As the years went by, many people came to the cemetery not to visit loved ones but simply to walk through the beautiful landscape, and the grounds were renamed Spring Grove Cemetery and Arboretum.

ghost story

Many ghost stories circulate about Spring Grove. The grounds are vast, and many areas are remote, so you'll find some places that are quite creepy.

The most famous ghost story involves the grave of an optometrist named C.C. Breuer. The story goes that when Breuer died, he asked that his eyes be removed from his body and placed into a bronze bust that was placed on the grave marker. The eyes in the bust actually do look real. Many people claim that when they walk near this bust, the eyes follow them, as if C.C. Breuer is watching them from beyond the grave. Unfortunately, most of this story isn't true. The eyes in the bust are made of glass and were chosen by Breuer himself because they closely resembled his own eyes. The fact that the eyes are glass doesn't explain the fact that they seem to follow people as they walk near the grave.

Skittish people who walk through haunted cemeteries are sometimes concerned that a corpse will reach up from beneath the ground and grab their legs. As terrifying as this sounds, it is almost unheard of that people report phenomena like this happening anywhere. Spring Grove Cemetery is one of those cemeteries, though, that people sometimes report being grabbed. A caretaker was working by himself and suddenly felt something grab his pants leg. He panicked and fled. Later, thinking more rationally about the situation, he returned to the site expecting to find that there was something on which he had caught his pants leg. To his horror, he found nothing in the area that could have caused this feeling.

Throughout the rest of the cemetery, people will report seeing figures that mysteriously disappear. People will hear voices and will be unable to find their source, and people will see strange white wolves that look at the witnesses before running away. These white wolves are thought to be harbingers of bad luck. According to rumors, people who see the wolves will experience some accident or other bad luck soon after their sighting.

visiting

On the one hand, it is unfortunate that this place closes to the public at night. Also, the staff and ownership of the cemetery do not support the rumors that the cemetery is haunted. They will tell you that the cemetery is not haunted, and they are not likely to support any large-scale investigation at any time.

On the other hand, most of the sightings that have been reported take place during regular daytime visiting hours. Another plus for ghost enthusiasts is that the place is so vast the cemetery could be somewhat busy and you may still never run into another living being. There are plenty of remote places to investigate.

If you are looking for the hotspots throughout the cemetery, go to: Lot 100—C.C. Breuer's final resting place; Section 87, Lot 20—Where the white wolves are most often seen; Section 53—Where the groundskeeper was grabbed; Section 16—Figures and voices are heard in this area, which is also the final resting place of the man whose death sparked the Courthouse Riots, William Kirk.

WESLEYAN CEMETERY

4003 Colerain Avenue, Cincinnati, OH 45223

directions

From I-75, take the I-74 West exit. From I-74, take the Colerain Avenue exit. At the end of the exit ramp, turn right onto Colerain Avenue. Wesleyan Cemetery will be on your right. The entrance is off Colerain.

history

In September of 1900, there was a fire at the Salvation Army orphanage on Front Street in downtown Cincinnati which was not only used to house orphans but was used as a kind of daycare center for the children of working parents in the area who could not afford any other kind of daycare. Some sort of gas leak caused an explosion that ignited the first floor of the orphanage. The children and workers were trapped on the third floor without any kind of fire escape or way out. Some people from the surrounding area were able to rescue a handful of the children from the burning building, but both workers, a man who tried to rush in to rescue his son and daughter, and six children died in the fire.

    The children were buried in Wesleyan Cemetery underneath a Salvation Army flag and a small white marble headstone. In recent years, the cemetery has decayed into a rather terrible state. Headstones were piled up haphazardly near trees. Some trees completely swallowed headstones into their trunks. Mausoleums were broken open. In the past couple of years, though, attempts have been made to restore the cemetery.

ghost story

A caretaker at the cemetery is convinced that several ghost children haunt the grounds. Even though the gates are closed at six p.m., the caretaker will sometimes hear children playing in the cemetery late into the night. He will look for these children and watch them run behind tombstones and then mysteriously disappear. He will hear laughter and children's voices, but he is never able to find anyone in the cemetery.

Sometimes the caretaker or passersby will hear children screaming from inside the cemetery, or they will see dark shadowy figures walking through the grounds at night. No one is ever found.

visiting

The cemetery is open to the public all day, and it is rarely busy. At six p.m., however, the gates close, and there is no way to access the cemetery. The house of the caretaker stands inside the gates. Even if you just wanted to stand outside the fence and look for shadowy figures at night, you could be in some danger. The neighborhood is not the safest in town, so you probably don't want to be standing out on the street at night, especially with expensive equipment.

WOODSIDE CEMETERY

1401 South Woodside Boulevard, Middletown, OH 45044

directions

Take I-75 north to exit 19, Union Center Boulevard. Turn left onto Union Center Boulevard, away from the movie theater and toward the restaurants. Follow this road for about three miles until you reach Princeton/Glendale Road. Turn right and follow this road for about six miles. Turn right onto Wright Brothers Memorial Hwy/Hamilton Middletown Road/OH-4 N. Follow this road for about six miles. Turn right onto Fourteenth Avenue/Martin Luther King Jr. Way. The cemetery is on your right.

history

The ghostly history of Woodside Cemetery dates back to the 1850s, about forty years before the land became a cemetery. Five men had robbed a bank in Indiana and had fled to Middletown. When the residents of Middletown learned that the bank robbers were hiding there, they formed a posse and cornered the men in the area that is today the cemetery. They lynched the five men, hanging them to death from a tree that sat in the center of where the cemetery is today.

By 1891, ghost stories had begun to circulate about the area, but officials wanted to build Woodside Cemetery at that location. They didn't want the cemetery to garner a reputation for being haunted by these men, so they decided that the best way to kill the ghostly rumors was to cut down the tree that the five men were hung from. They cut down the tree and built the cemetery there in 1891. The ghost stories didn't stop.

ghost story

Many people still see the hanging tree in Woodside Cemetery despite the fact that the tree was taken down more than a hundred years ago. It remains the only ghost tree in southwestern Ohio.

Not only will people see the non-existent tree, but people will see the entire lynching scene replay itself within the bounds of the cemetery. At night, the dark grounds will come alive with movement. Five figures will hang limply from the ghostly tree. Other times, people will see the whole posse surrounding the tree and will hear voices and commotion coming from within the cemetery itself.

It seems like the cemetery's plan to remove the tree in order to stop the ghost stories failed. The remnants of the lynching that occurred here in the mid 1800s still haunt this location to this day.

visiting

No one is quite certain anymore exactly where the hanging tree stood. Most of the sightings of the tree occur after dark near the Fourteenth Avenue entrance. Since the cemetery is closed after dark, it makes sense that most of the sightings occur near an entrance. The best way to witness this ghostly reenactment is to stand near the Fourteenth Avenue entrance long after dark and look into the cemetery for movement.

SECTION II

roads and bridges

Haunted roads and bridges

are some of the most popular places

to search for ghosts because these areas are

so accessible. Roads don't close at night.

Roads aren't located on private property.

But while you are able to go to these roads

and bridges at any time of the night without

fear of legal problems, a different type of

fear tends to take over.

BLOME ROAD BRIDGE

Blome Road and Spooky Hollow Road, Indian Hill, OH 45243

directions

Take I-71 north until you reach OH-126, the Ronald Reagan Highway. Take Ronald Reagan east toward Montgomery. Less than a half mile down the road, take the Montgomery Road exit and turn right onto Montgomery Road. Less than a quarter mile down Montgomery, turn right onto Findley Lane. Then turn left onto Spooky Ridge Lane. About a quarter mile down this road, turn right onto Spooky Hollow Road. Continue straight on this road until it curves up to the left. Continue to go straight onto Blome (pronounced *bloom*) Road. The bridge is not far. You can't miss it. It will be one of the creepiest bridges you've ever seen.

history

This bridge in the historic village of Indian Hill was built in 1888. Since it is only one lane wide, a series of accidents have occurred on the bridge. One incident involved a car speeding toward the bridge and swerving to avoid an oncoming car. The swerving car dove headlong into the wooded creek area beside the bridge and all inside were killed. A series of other accidents have reputedly occurred on the bridge, but it is difficult to tell if they are true. For that reason, I have included the most famous reputed tragedy of this bridge in the ghost story section of this chapter.

Today the bridge is still only one lane wide, but there is a stop sign on either side of the bridge. The sign makes it safer, but there are still those drivers who disregard the sign.

ghost story

The most popular ghost story that supposedly occurs at this bridge involves a hit-and-run accident. A pregnant woman was walking across the bridge when, from the opposite direction, a car raced toward her, unaware that she was on the bridge. It hit her and knocked her over the side of the bridge to her death. The driver stopped the car, and he stepped out to see if she was okay. She wasn't. She was dead. In a panic, he rushed back to his car. As he scrambled into his car, a penny somehow rolled out of the car and off the bridge toward the body of the woman. According to legend, if you turn off your car on the bridge, roll down the window, and throw a penny off the bridge, within three minutes the penny will come back and hit your car.

People also claim they hear voices coming from the nearby woods. They attribute the voices to the accident in which the car swerved into the creek. People also have claimed that while driving across the bridge their cars have been hit hard by an unseen object. When the driver checks the car for what had hit it, he or she cannot find anything and can find no damage anywhere.

visiting

Late at night, not many cars go down this remote stretch of road. Further, there are stop signs on both sides of the bridge, and other drivers have a reasonable amount of time to react when they see a car stopped on the bridge. The bridge, however, is not without dangers. Sometimes cars will go across the bridge, especially late at night, without heeding the stop signs. If you choose to stop on the bridge and turn off your car, make sure you keep your headlights on so other drivers can see you. I keep the car running whenever I go to this location so that if I see headlights cresting the hill in front of me or behind me, I can quickly cross the bridge and allow them to pass. This bridge is not difficult to investigate, but be careful.

MIAMITOWN BRIDGE
Harrison Avenue and State Route 128, Miamitown, OH 45041

directions
Take I-74 west to exit 7 (Hamilton/Cleves/128). Turn right onto 128, toward the gas stations and Wendy's. You will go through Miamitown and will get to a traffic light at Harrison Avenue. Turn right on Harrison to cross the haunted bridge.

history
This is the fourth bridge to span this part of the Great Miami River. The first one was a covered bridge that was torn down in 1863 to prevent the Confederate cavalry led by John Hunt Morgan from crossing it. The second one was built in 1894 and was a big steel bridge where at least a couple of fatalities occurred. The first fatality occurred when a hay wagon was going over the bridge in the 1930s and a man on the back of the wagon was taken by surprise by a sudden swerve, falling into the river and drowning. The second fatality occurred as construction work was being done on the bridge in the 1950s. The decking of the bridge had been torn up and the bridge was closed. A man got drunk at the Flicker Inn on Harrison Avenue and tried to drive home. He didn't realize that the bridge was out, so he started to drive across it, his

tires remarkably able to stay on the two steel beams which still crossed the river. About halfway across the bridge, a tire slipped off the beam and his car became stuck. He stepped out of his car to see what had happened, but, because of the lack of decking, he fell into the river below and drowned.

In 1989, plans were made to construct a new bridge, one that would be more like an overpass, an extension of the road itself. In order to build this structure, however, they had to build a temporary bridge to carry traffic while the old bridge was torn down and the new one was built. In May 1989, there had been many storms, and the river level had risen significantly. Debris in the river hit the wooden pylons that supported the bridge. At 5:26 p.m. on May 26, 1989, the temporary span of the Miamitown Bridge collapsed. Officially, one car went down with the bridge, and two people died in the collapse. Witnesses claim that a red truck also went down with the bridge but the red truck was never found, and no one ever reported a red truck missing.

ghost story

With such a long history of tragedy, it's no wonder that several ghosts have taken up residence on this span of steel and asphalt over the Great Miami River. The most famous and widely reported ghost here is supposedly the driver of the red truck, who everyone saw go down with the bridge but whose vehicle and body were never found. The ghost appears in the form of a glowing white apparition that begins crossing the bridge from the east toward Miamitown. As the ghost crosses the bridge, it slowly starts to dissipate. It never makes it all the way across the bridge without disappearing.

While this glowing white apparition is the most famous ghost, other strange things are reported. People standing on the bridge will often see shadowy figures start to walk across. Almost as quickly as they appear, these figures will vanish as if they were never there and were nothing more than a trick of the eyes.

visiting

This bridge can be visited at any time of the day or night. You can either drive across, or you can park in Miamitown and walk out onto a sidewalk on the south side of the bridge. This sidewalk is always open and is completely safe at all hours since there is a concrete barricade between this sidewalk and the roadway and a large fence between the sidewalk and the river below.

PEACEFUL VALLEY

Near the intersection of Stonelick-Williams Corner Road and
Baizhiser Lane, Goshen, OH 45122

directions

The area known as Peaceful Valley includes land along SR-28 and the area just south
of it along the Stonelick Creek. To get to SR-28, take I-71 north to I-275 east to exit
57. Head east along SR-28. When you get to SR-132 in the city of Goshen, turn right.
Follow this road (it becomes Williams Corner Road) until you get to a road called
Stonelick Williams Corner Road. Turn right; the haunted bridge will be down the
road a little ways.

You can also take the US-50 Milford exit off I-275. Take 50 to the east until you
get to Stonelick-Williams Corner Road and turn left onto the road. This way you get
to the haunted bridge quicker, but you skip the rest of the Peaceful Valley.

history

There's not a lot of dark history from the area to account for the ghostly activity here,
but many rumors exist of extensive cult practices performed near Stonelick Road.
The covered bridge, which sits on this road, was built in 1878, making it the most
recently constructed covered bridge in Clermont County. The area is quite rural with
few houses around.

ghost story

Despite the lack of documented tragedy on which to base a ghost story, Peaceful Valley
does not live up to its name. It is a scary place to go.

One of the stranger ghost stories involves a small farmhouse near the covered
bridge. Legend says that as you drive by this farmhouse, there will be an equal number

of lights lit as there are passengers in your car. No one is quite sure exactly which house it is supposed to be, but I guess you could look for the farmhouse that has the equal number of lights as passengers in your car and find it that way.

The bridge is also said to be haunted. People will see figures and hear voices on it. According to legend, you need to stop your car on the bridge for many of these strange things to occur. The most famous legend is that if you turn off your car on the bridge and flash your lights three times, you will see a man hang himself in a nearby tree. The legend says that you will not be able to restart your car until the man appears.

Most of the reports from the area involve the cult that is said to practice in the area. They are said to hang out near the bridge, and if they catch you stopped on or near the bridge, they will chase you away in a pickup truck. They will ride the pickup truck right up on your bumper with the high beams on, and then will mysteriously disappear without any apparent place to turn off. Sometimes, these cult members supposedly open your doors and try to drag you out of your car.

visiting

It is legal to be in this area after dark, but it is probably not legal to stop on the bridge and flash your lights. There are cameras positioned all over the bridge, and there are many police officers who patrol the area nightly, making sure that people aren't creating disturbances or breaking laws. Sometimes these officers will simply chase cars out of the area without turning on their lights or sirens. This could explain some of the stories where people are chased from the valley by vehicles.

However, there could be further danger than being chased away by cops. People have reported that when they are stopped on the bridge, unseen figures will open the car doors and reach in to try to grab the people and the keys. When the assaulted car starts to flee, the pickup truck will chase them for many miles around the city.

I'm not one who jumps easily at ghosts. I looked at the farmhouses in the area by the bridge and sure enough there was one with two lights on and there were two people in the car. I don't know if it was the right one or not, but it didn't scare me. When I stopped on the bridge, I wasn't scared of ghosts, despite the strange stories of voices and figures. But when I was on the bridge, my windows were most of the way up, I triple-checked to make sure that my door was locked, and, even though the legend dictates that the car needs to be off to find the hanging man, I kept the car on in case I needed to make a quick escape. Maybe that's why I didn't see the hanging man.

THE SCREAMING BRIDGE

6300 Maud Hughes Road, Liberty Township, OH 45044

directions

Take I-75 north to Cincinnati-Dayton Road (exit 21). Turn left onto Cincinnati-Dayton Road. Follow this road for a couple of miles. It will eventually change its name to Maud Hughes Road. The Screaming Bridge is on Maud Hughes Road. Once you follow this road for two miles, it will appear to dead-end into Princeton Road. Turn right onto Princeton Road. Then take the first left, which will be the continuation of Maud Hughes Road. The first bridge that you come to will be the Screaming Bridge. It crosses railroad tracks about twenty feet off the ground.

history

The bridge that crosses the railroad tracks at Maud Hughes Road was originally steel with a steel deck. Whenever a car would go across the bridge, it would sound like someone was screaming. This is where its name originated. However, there have been tragedies on or near this bridge that could produce some human screaming.

Many car accidents have happened here. The road turns sharply and blindly before the bridge, so if a car comes fast around the turn and someone is stopped on the bridge, there will be an accident.

There are also rumors of many suicides on this bridge. The most common story involves a young woman who got pregnant and had a child out of wedlock. She took the baby to the Screaming Bridge and threw it to its death before hanging herself from the bridge.

There have been train accidents near the bridge as well. One happened in 1976, when a northbound train carrying rails was approaching a southbound train. The rails somehow came loose and pointed out the side, working like a jouster's lance toward the oncoming train. The engineer of the oncoming train was impaled and the brakeman was seriously injured. Another accident occurred in 1909 when the boiler on the train mysteriously exploded underneath the bridge. The engineer and brakeman survived the initial explosion, but they were slowly scalded to death by the water from the boiler. Other passengers also died in the accident.

ghost story

Many ghost stories are told about the bridge. A common one is that screams are still heard coming from the bridge even though the decking no longer makes the screaming sound when a car crosses. People also have heard voices and seen figures that appear to be crying. Sometimes people under the bridge will see two legs come over the side, as if someone has just hung him or herself. When they rush to the top to see what happened, the bridge is empty.

There also are stories that involve the train accidents that occurred here. People will see men dressed in trainman uniforms walking down the tracks. These figures simply vanish or will look up at the witnesses first before vanishing. People also have seen ghostly train cars on the tracks underneath the bridge or sitting on the nearby tracks. The train cars slowly dissipate into the night.

visiting

Visiting this site is not easy. First of all, I can't stress enough how dangerous it is to stop your car on the bridge itself. There are trees on all of the corners, and it's impossible to see a stopped vehicle. If someone comes around the corner late at night, they are not likely to see you in time.

Also, there is nowhere to park nearby. There are only private houses and driveways along the road for about a mile in either direction. I have asked someone to drive me to the site, and I got out of the car in one of the straight sections before the bridge. I then walked to the bridge to investigate and take photographs while my ride drove down the road and waited before turning around to pick me up.

Another time, I stopped at the police station about a mile away and asked if I could park in their lot while I went to the bridge. They gave me permission, and I walked down the tracks to the bridge. I did this during the day. I don't know how accommodating they will be at night. They did tell me that the tracks are on public property so there was nothing they could do to stop me from walking down the tracks.

This area is in a safe part of town, but the underside of the bridge is covered with graffiti and I am always a little uncomfortable being anywhere at night where vandals frequent. Finally, the tracks are still in use. Keep an eye out for trains.

SPOOK HOLLOW BRIDGE

Corner of Corwin Road and Middletown Road, Oregonia, OH 45054

directions

Take I-71 north from Cincinnati until you reach exit 36, the Wilmington Road exit. Turn left at Wilmington Road, which will make a sharp turn to the right and change its name to Corwin Road. At Race Street, Corwin will make a sharp right turn and then a sharp left but stay on it. A few miles past Race Street, take a left onto Middletown Road. The haunted bridge is immediately past this turn. It is a large covered bridge; you can't miss it.

history

The dark history behind this bridge involves an auto accident. The story goes that a car full of teenagers came around the corner and headed toward the bridge at a very high speed. The 90-degree turn before the bridge proved too difficult to make at such speed, and they plummeted from the bridge into the icy river below. Everyone in the car was killed, but a young woman in the car met an especially grisly end. She was decapitated and, according to legend, her head was never found.

ghost story

The bridge is haunted by the ghost of the woman who died in the terrible car wreck. Witnesses will see an apparition of a headless woman who roams the area on or near the bridge. The legend says that she is constantly looking for her lost head.

Other stories involve the head itself. The stories go that if you stop your car on the bridge at midnight, you will either see the head or the head will drop onto your car.

Beyond the stories of the headless woman, people will see other dark figures roaming around this bridge. People report hearing the sounds of sobbing or of a car accident—even when no one is there.

visiting

The only obstacle to visiting this site is its remoteness. It is located in the little town of Oregonia. Otherwise, there isn't much that will prevent you from searching for ghosts here. The bridge is open all night, and there isn't very much traffic on the bridge after dark. The traffic that does cross the bridge has to stop and turn before they get to the bridge, so even if you are stopped on the bridge and the oncoming car doesn't see you, they will be going slow enough to stop in plenty of time to avoid an accident. It seems that the only scary thing about visiting this site is the ghost itself.

BUELL ROAD
Buell Road, Cincinnati, OH 45251

directions
To get to this road, you take I-75 north to I-275 west to the Hamilton Avenue/US-127 exit, exit 36, between Colerain Avenue and Winton Road. Turn right to head north on Hamilton Avenue then take your first left onto Houston Road. Follow Houston Road until you reach Pippin Road and take a left on Pippin. Buell Road will be on your right, near Triple Creek Park. The haunted area is about halfway down the road when it levels out and becomes straight for about a quarter mile. You will know you are in the right place if you see a cross on the left side of the road.

history
Though the dark history of this road doesn't match the strange ghost story that goes along with it, the history is certainly worth mentioning. For some reason, there have been many car accidents along this road. In 2007, there was a tragic accident on the stretch of road where the ghost supposedly haunts. Four teenagers were driving home from school down Buell one day at very high speeds and lost control of their car. The accident killed all four people in the car. Today there is a little roadside memorial at the site of the accident.

The ghost most often mentioned is that of a boy who rides a bicycle, but I could find no historic records of anyone matching that description who was killed anywhere near the site of the haunting.

ghost story

The ghost of Buell Road, if the stories are true, is an especially dangerous one. The legend says that in order to encounter this ghost, you first need to summon it by stopping your car on the straight section of the road and flashing your lights three times. After flashing your lights, turn them off. At this time, the ghost is supposed to appear in the form of a small boy on a bicycle who slowly comes around the curve behind your car. While this ghost story might seem rather innocent, the legend goes on to say that if you don't turn your headlights back on by the time the boy reaches your car, you will die exactly seven days later.

visiting

Beyond the obvious danger of dying seven days after you see this ghost, there are more immediate dangers when testing this legend—most of all, traffic on the road. From time to time cars zip along at high speeds down this road in the middle of the night. If you are stopped in the middle of the road flashing your lights, it is very possible that an oncoming vehicle will be unable to stop in time. So keep an eye out for the boy on the bike, but keep a closer eye out for oncoming headlights of actual vehicles who won't take seven days to kill you.

BUFFALO RIDGE ROAD

Corner of Buffalo Ridge Road and Zion Road, Cleves, OH 45002

directions

Take I-74 west until you get to the Harrison Pike/Rybolt Road exit. Turn right onto Harrison Pike and follow the road until you get to Wesselman Road. Take a left onto Wesselman and follow it for about a mile or so. Buffalo Ridge Road will be on your right.

history

In the woods up on the ridge, you'll see the foundations of a ruined building. These are the remains of an old planetarium that the Cincinnati Astronomical Society attempted to build from stone left over from the Cincinnati Chamber of Commerce fire in 1911. The funding fell through on the project before it was completed, so the foundation was simply left in the woods. This foundation still sits among weeds in the woods alongside tons of finished marble work that was moved from the site of the Chamber of Commerce.

Many car accidents have occurred here, usually the result of teenagers racing down the hilly, curvy road. In the 1950s, a school bus crashed and several children were killed. At the top of the ridge, there is a county park named Mitchell Memorial Forest, which was created through land donated by a man named William Morris Mitchell. He donated the land with the stipulation that it would be made into a park as a memorial to his deceased parents. He also stipulated that none of the land be sold off to the public.

ghost story

Many ghost stories circulate about this creepy road. One posits that the foundation ruins in the woods are from a crematorium that burned to the ground, and the spirits of those who were burned roam the woods as angry shadowy figures. Part of this story isn't true. The "crematorium" is actually the planetarium. People do see shadow figures roaming the woods, however. These figures could be linked to satanic activity. People have found small animals that appear to have been killed ritualistically. Perhaps these satanic ceremonies have kicked up some evil entities.

The most famous ghost story involves a white van that will tailgate cars driving down this road at night. The white van disappears suddenly, though there is no place where it could have turned off the road. Another story involves the school bus accident that occurred in the 1950s. It's said that if you park your car near the top of the ridge, near Zion Road, and you let your windows fog up, children's handprints will appear in the condensation.

Also, there is a pond visible from Buffalo Ridge Road that was once beautiful and clear and was part of the land donated by William Morris Mitchell. A nearby homeowner offered the county a lot of money to annex the pond to his property, and the county sold it despite Mitchell's stipulation that the land never be sold to the public. Today the pond is dirty and turbulent, and some locals claim that Mitchell's ghost haunts the pond.

Beyond these stories, people sometimes will see an albino wolf with red eyes at the crest of the ridge near Zion Road. People who live in the houses on Buffalo Ridge Road will hear phantom car wrecks. Finally, there is a house near the Wesselman Road side of Buffalo Ridge Road that is reportedly haunted by a witch. Despite the fact that the house is clearly abandoned and electricity has not gone to the house for ages, people see lights inside and the silhouette of an old woman in the windows.

visiting

It is safe and legal to drive on Buffalo Ridge Road all night long, looking for any kind of ghostly activity. If you want to stop the car to let the windows fog up for the ghostly kids from the school bus accident, make sure you pull off the road first. There is a nice little spot to pull off near Zion Road. Don't pull into anyone's driveway, and don't stop in the middle of the road or you may cause an accident.

The ruins of the planetarium are a little more difficult to visit legally. The ruins are in an area of the Mitchell Memorial Forest that is closed to the public. The easiest way to get to the ruins is a trail about a quarter mile east of Zion Road. Unfortunately, the trail is clearly marked with a "no trespassing" sign, which means you will be arrested if you are caught there. When I went into the woods, I wrote to the Hamilton County Parks asking permission to take photographs for a book I was writing. They granted permission but required that I print out documentation in case park rangers stopped me. It is well worth going into the woods to see the ruins but get official permission before you go.

CLERMONT COUNTY'S DEAD MAN'S CURVE

Intersection of SR-125 and SR-222, Bethel, OH 45106

directions

Take I-471 south to I-275 east. Take I-275 to exit 65, Beechmont Avenue/Amelia. Turn right at the end of the exit to head eastbound on SR-125. About nine and a half miles down the road, you will reach the intersection of SR-125 and SR-222. The haunted section of road is between this intersection and the intersection of SR-125 and Bantam Road. The road has been straightened out considerably since the days when it was the dangerous curve, but it is this section that is reputed to be haunted.

history

This stretch of road has earned the name Dead Man's Curve. As far back as the late 1800s, horse-drawn carriages would slide off the road at this point, causing fatalities. When cars replaced the carriages, the accidents continued. Perhaps the most famous one occurred in October of 1969 when five teenagers in a Chevy Impala were hit by a car that had lost control on the curve. All five teenagers were killed in the crash.

Due to the high rate of accidents, authorities finally decided to fix the road so that it was no longer as dangerous. Today, there is hardly any indication that there was a sharp turn capable of causing numerous accidents—except for the ghosts.

ghost story

There are several creepy stories that circulate about SR-125 between the intersection with SR-222 and the intersection with Bantam Road. People will often see ghost cars along this stretch, including the ghostly image of a Chevy Impala like the one in which the five teenagers were killed. Other times people will see the ghostly image of the car that struck the Impala. Carriages and antique cars are also seen moving along the road, only to disappear mysteriously into nothingness.

Perhaps the most famous ghost of the area is that of the "Faceless Hitchhiker," a moniker that the ghost has attained through its many sightings. This hitchhiker is often seen emerging from the tree line near Dead Man's Curve. When those who are driving by look at him, they see that he has no facial features. Other times, this same faceless man will chase cars that are stopped at the traffic light at the intersection of 125 and 222.

visiting

According to legends, the best time to encounter ghosts in the area is between 1:20 a.m. and 1:40 a.m. This is when the faceless hitchhiker is most often seen, and it is also a time when you can encounter the ghost cars. Since it is so late at night, you won't have to worry too much about other traffic on the road. The only other traffic you may have to deal with is that of other ghost enthusiasts looking for a glimpse of the frightening faceless hitchhiker.

HARRISON AVENUE'S DEAD MAN'S CURVE

Just west of the intersection of Harrison Avenue and
State Route 128, Cleves, OH 45002

directions

Take I-74 west to exit 7. Turn right (north) onto 128, toward the gas stations and
Wendy's. Take 128 through Miamitown until you get to Harrison Avenue. Turn left
onto Harrison Avenue. From where the road begins to curve in front of the Village
Pump Antique store up to the point where it straightens out at the top of the hill is
what the locals know as Dead Man's Curve.

history

Many accidents have occurred on this stretch of road between Miamitown and
Harrison. Most of these accidents happened in the mid-1900s. During this time,
Harrison Avenue was the major artery of traffic through the area since the Interstate
Highway System had not yet been created. At least fifty-two serious injuries or fatalities
have occurred in vehicular accidents going up or coming down Dead Man's Curve.

Probably the most spectacular of these accidents involved a molasses truck that was coming down Dead Man's Curve toward the Miamitown Bridge in 1953. It didn't make the last turn and barreled into what was at that time the post office at the corner of Harrison and 128. It caught fire. One man rushed into the burning post office in a futile attempt to help the truck driver, who was pinned in his truck. He was alive and conscious but could not get out, and the Good Samaritan could not help him. Eventually the propane tanks heating the molasses exploded, and the entire block burned to the ground. The only fatality was the truck driver, who, since he was alive and conscious, most likely burned to death.

ghost story

A phantom hitchhiker haunts Dead Man's Curve. The story goes that if you are driving up or down Dead Man's Curve, you sometimes will see a man hitchhiking on the side of the road. Whether or not your original intention was to pick the man up, as you get closer and closer to him, you are filled with more and more of a sense of dread and fear. By the time any cars get next to him, they are so terrified that they speed away. No one ever stops to pick him up. The few people brave enough to slow down and look at the man see that he is very badly burned. They even sometimes report that the flesh is hanging from his face and from his hands. Perhaps this is the ghost of the man who burned to death in the truck accident in 1953.

visiting

There is nothing stopping you from looking for this ghost all you want. You can drive up and down this road all night long. I do not know what direction of the road that the phantom hitchhiker prefers. The reports that I have collected seem to be from both sides, so you have an equal chance of seeing him when coming down the hill and when going up.

The one thing to keep in mind on this road is to be careful. The locals don't call it Dead Man's Curve for nothing. The hills are steep and the turns are sharp. It is hard to make it up and down these curves if you are unfamiliar with the area, especially after dark, so take special care to stay safe when driving the road.

EAST MIAMI RIVER ROAD

Corner of East Miami River Road and Buffalo Ridge Road,
Cleves, OH 45247

directions

Take I-74 to exit 7 (SR-128/Hamilton/Cleves). Turn right (north) onto 128 toward the
BP and the Wendy's. This will take you through Miamitown. Turn right at Harrison
Avenue at the light. This will take you across the Miamitown Bridge. About a half-
mile down the road, take the first road on the right. This road is East Miami River
Road. Several miles down the road near the intersection with Buffalo Ridge Road is
the haunted section of the road.

history

This section of the road is quite dark and creepy at night. It runs alongside the Great
Miami River and eventually will take you to the Edgewater drag-racing strip.

There have been houses along this road for many years, meaning that many people have died in these old houses. There is one tragic story from the area that seems to partially echo the strange ghost story here. There was a woman who had a boyfriend, and together they had two sons. According to legend, her boyfriend finally proposed, but unfortunately, as she was driving home one day along I-275, she got into a terrible accident at the overpass above East Miami River Road. When rescue workers sifted through the wreckage, they discovered that the woman had been decapitated.

Her boyfriend and two sons were living in a trailer near the intersection of East Miami River Road and Buffalo Ridge Road. Somehow a fire started in the trailer. The father was able to escape, but both boys perished in the flames.

ghost story

The ghost appears only at night, and, according to legend, appears only on the anniversary of the woman's death. The road is quite long and straight and is lined by many houses. Since there are so many houses and no sidewalks, people from the area often walk in the road. The ghost takes the form of a person walking down the road, but you'll realize quickly that this is not a normal person from the area. The ghost is always seen wearing a white wedding dress. She also is missing her head.

People say that this is the ghost of the woman who was decapitated in the car accident on I-275. When they discovered that she had been decapitated, they searched for her head in the wreckage but were unable to find it. People suggest that the headless woman in the wedding dress is searching for her missing head on the anniversary of her death.

visiting

While no one has been able to tell me the exact date that this ghost is seen year after year, witnesses do agree that she appears either late in the summer or early in the fall. In my opinion, this is the best time of year to go looking. Also, the ghost is seen most often near the intersection with Buffalo Ridge Road, and she is seen only at night.

This ghost is often seen by passing motorists, and the road is open and relatively straight and level. It is reasonably safe to drive up and down this road all night looking for the ghost.

HAMILTON NEW LONDON ROAD

Hamilton New London Road, Hamilton, OH 45013

directions

Take I-75 north to I-275 west. Take I-275 to the Colerain Avenue exit (exit 33) and head north on US-27/Colerain Avenue. Follow this road for about five and a half miles until you get into Ross at the intersection of US-27 and SR-128. Take the ramp and turn right onto 128. Follow 128 for a little more than 6 ½ miles. When you come to the bridge to Hamilton on your right, New London Road will be on your left. The haunted section of the road begins at this point and ends at the top of the hill.

history

The historical context behind this ghost involves a doctor who once lived on New London Road in an upscale district of Hamilton. Since he was a doctor, he was known to be quite health conscious and would spend his early mornings jogging up and then back down the big hill going up the road from the river. One day, during one of these jogs, the doctor suffered a fatal heart attack and died alongside the road. His body was found by a passing motorist. I have not found a record of this fatality and am unsure if the story has any basis in fact. My sense is that the doctor's death occurred—if it really did occur—sometime in the 1970s. Or perhaps that's when the story began to circulate.

ghost story

A rather creepy ghost story is often reported on New London Road in the area near where the doctor died. The story goes that sometimes when you start driving up the hill from the river away from Hamilton, you will pass a man jogging alongside the road. The man will wave at you as you drive past him and then will quickly disappear in your rearview mirror. At this point, most passing motorists wouldn't think that anything strange was going on. Drivers pass joggers all the time so the witnesses don't even give it a second thought until they reach the top of the hill.

At the top of the hill, the witnesses are surprised to see the same jogger that they had passed long ago standing at the top of the hill, waving at them. As the jogger waves, he disappears into thin air.

visiting

There are actually two times of day when people report seeing this apparition. One is early in the morning near dawn, the time when the doctor would jog up and down the hill. The other time is late at night. Drivers will be a little confused when they see a jogger on the road at that time of night and then downright terrified when the jogger vanishes before their eyes.

The road is straight and safe to drive up and down at any time. The only reports that I have heard of the jogger involve the car driving up the hill; the jogger is never seen on the way down.

HIGHWAY TO HEAVEN

US-27 between Ross and Oxford, OH 45013

directions

Take I-75 north to I-275 west. Take I-275 to the Colerain Avenue exit. Take Colerain Avenue to the north. The road will become a two-lane highway until you reach the town of Ross. Continue to follow SR-27 through Ross. The fabled "Highway to Heaven" is SR-27 between Ross and Oxford.

history

This stretch of highway between Ross and Oxford has a very dark reputation. It is considered one of the more dangerous roads in America, a fact that is hard to imagine after having driven the road, which is flat and straight and seems quite safe. Its reputation, however, is not completely unfounded. There have been thousands of car accidents along this road, hundreds of them fatal. These accidents are often caused by both impatient drivers and the deceptiveness of the road itself. Many people who drive this stretch of road are going from Cincinnati to Miami University in Oxford. They stay on this road for many miles, and if they are caught behind a slow driver, there is little recourse other than to pass. But the road is deceptively hilly while it appears rather straight and flat. Shallow hills tend to hide oncoming vehicles, and many cars will often attempt to pass along this road and encounter oncoming traffic. A head-on collision at the speeds these vehicles are going often results in fatal accidents. Roadside crosses dot the landscape all along this stretch of road.

ghost story

The ghost story from this road is rather strange. The story goes that if you are driving down SR-27 between Ross and Oxford, at some point you may see a single motorcycle headlight heading directly toward you in your lane. At the last second, when you think that the motorcycle will hit you head-on, it suddenly takes flight and ramps up into the air above your car and disappears into the night sky.

visiting

You can legally drive this road anytime. There is no one place where the ghostly motorcycle most often appears, and it has been seen on both the northbound and southbound sides of the highway. You'll want to keep a sharp lookout anywhere between Ross and Oxford.

When searching for this ghost, keep in mind that this is a dangerous road. It doesn't appear to be dangerous as you are driving down it, but cars can appear out of nowhere. If you are looking for this ghost, drive down the road as much as you like—just be careful and don't pass other cars unless you are absolutely sure that there are no oncoming vehicles.

LICK ROAD

Lick Road, Cincinnati, OH 45251

directions

Take I-75 north to I-275 west. From I-275, take the Colerain Avenue exit and turn right (away from Bob Evans) on SR27. You will take this road past the Rumpke dump until you see an exit for Kemper Road. Turn east (right) onto Kemper Road. Keep an eye out for Lick Road on your left. Lick Road will stretch for about a half mile before dead-ending into the supposedly haunted area of the road.

history

The history of the road itself is not difficult to determine. It was once a part of a road called Bank Lick Road, which stretched from Kemper Road all the way into Butler County through what is today the Richardson Nature Preserve. A bridge that crossed a small creek just past the current end of Lick Road was deemed unsuitable for vehicular traffic, so the road was simply closed down and turned into a nature preserve.

There is another, darker history to the area that is a little harder to pin down. The stories are always changing as to exactly what occurred at the end of the road to cause ghosts to appear there. The most popular story is that there was a young girl standing on the bridge behind Lick Road with her boyfriend. For some reason, he got upset with her and ended up killing her. Another story says that the young girl was waiting for her boyfriend on the bridge and he never showed up so she hung herself there.

Still another says that as the young girl was waiting for her boyfriend, a couple of men found her and raped and killed her on the bridge.

The only story for which I could find any historic truth concerns a sixteen-year-old girl named Linda Dyer, who was hitchhiking in 1976 and was picked up by two men who took her to the secluded end of Lick Road and raped and murdered her there. Her body was later discovered underneath a small bridge very close to where Lick Road is today.

ghost story

Even though the only murder I could uncover was that of Linda Dyer, the consensus among those who know about this ghost claims that her name is Amy. There is a street sign warning of a curve in the road that says the name 'Amy' in graffiti as one approaches Lick Road on Kemper, but it is impossible to tell whether the graffiti on the sign predated the naming of the ghost or if the ghost was named as a result of the sign. It is possible that the graffiti on the sign was done by some delinquent trying to impress a girlfriend and that the name on the sign has nothing to do with the ghost.

The most famous paranormal tale about the area near the dead end of Lick is that if you sit in your vehicle and let the windows fog up, the word 'help' will appear on your windows. This isn't the only story, however. There are many others focused on this lonely stretch of road. People have seen dark figures disappear into the forest. They have heard crying and screaming coming from the woods. Glowing balls of light have encircled frightened witnesses, and footsteps often have been heard when no one is walking around.

visiting

Just a year or two ago, one could visit this place and try to experience the paranormal, but the stories have become so popular that the road has become a hangout at night. Unfortunately, many of the recent visitors are young and they come to party. The police now patrol the area nightly, which is a mixed blessing. On the one hand, they have strongly discouraged teenagers from holding their drinking parties there, but on the other hand, if you are looking for ghosts, the police will question you and ask you to leave. There also is a curfew in the area, so if you are younger than eighteen and the police come down to the end of the road, the consequences may be more severe than simply being asked to leave.

Also, the Richardson Nature Preserve is closed at dark, so if you venture back to the bridge after dark, you are trespassing on government property.

LOVELAND MADEIRA ROAD

Loveland Madeira Road, Cincinnati, OH 45243

directions

Take I-71 north to I-275 east. Take I-275 to the Loveland/Indian Hill exit. Turn right off the exit onto Loveland Madeira Road. At this point you are heading toward Madeira. When you reach Indian Hill, turn around and head back toward Loveland in order to encounter this ghost.

history

This road is long and relatively straight. It extends from Madeira, through Indian Hill, into Loveland. In the 1960s through the early 1980s, teenagers used to have drag races on this road late at night. Unfortunately, these races ended in disaster at least once. A young man was killed when he lost control of his car and crashed into one of the many trees that line the road.

ghost story

One ghost story is often told about this particular road. If you are going the speed limit or under the speed limit while on this road, headed from Madeira to Loveland, you will sometimes see the headlights of a car come speeding up behind you. These lights will come closer and closer to you at very high speeds. At the last second, when you feel that the car could not possibly stop in time, the car loses control and swerves to the right, appearing to crash into a tree beside the road. When you stop your car to see the wreckage, you notice that there is no wreckage; there is no sign that a car had ever been behind you.

visiting

Testing out this ghost story tends to work best late at night. It's quite safe to drive down this road since there are few sharp turns, and it is relatively flat. Beyond this, the legend requires that you drive at or under the speed limit for the ghost to appear, so this makes testing this legend even safer.

MOUNT HEALTHY

Any alley near Hamilton Avenue, Mount Healthy, OH 45231

directions

Take I-75 north to I-275 west. Take I-275 to the Hamilton Avenue/US-127 exit. Take a left and follow Hamilton Avenue to the south. This will take you directly into Mount Healthy. The remote alleys between the buildings in the downtown area are where this phenomenon occurs most often.

history

Up until 1849, Mt. Healthy was known as Mt. Pleasant. In 1849 a terrible cholera epidemic struck the entire Cincinnati area—with the exception of Mt. Pleasant. The community was proud that they avoided the epidemic but fearful that people from the surrounding area would flee to Mt. Pleasant and bring the disease with them. And so the community quarantined itself from the outside world. When trains carrying visitors would stop in town, the residents of Mt. Pleasant would instruct them to move on. The quarantine continued until the epidemic ended. In honor of their health during the epidemic and because there was already another town in Ohio called Mt. Pleasant, residents changed the name to Mt. Healthy.

ghost story

It is said that in Mt. Healthy you can sometimes hear train whistles echoing throughout the town at night. This may not seem strange, but no trains come anywhere near Mt. Healthy anymore. There is no reason you should hear these train whistles. Some people believe the ghost trains are full of the spirits of those who were denied entry to Mt. Healthy during the cholera epidemic. They have come back to haunt the town that denied them access and health in life.

visiting

It is okay to visit Mt. Healthy at night in order to search for ghosts. It is a safe neighborhood, and there are no laws that prevent people from walking the streets at night as long as they are not creating any kind of disturbance.

The train whistles supposedly are heard most often in the back-alley areas of the town. These are the places that you should visit if you hope to hear the phantom whistles. Also, the whistles occur most often at night, so you will want to go when it is dark, after the sounds of traffic have died off.

NARROWS ROAD

3700 Narrows Road, Erlanger, KY 41018

directions

From downtown Cincinnati, take I-75 south until you hit I-275 in Kentucky at Erlanger. Take I-275 east and follow that until you reach the Turkeyfoot Road exit (exit 82). Turn right onto Turkeyfoot Road and stay on it for almost three miles, and then turn left onto Brightleaf Boulevard. Your first left will be Narrows Road. The ghost stories seem to occur exclusively down near the dead-end side of the road.

history

Narrows Road dead-ends into a secluded part of a wooded area, but up until about a decade ago, it continued through those woods all the way to Turkeyfoot Road. The ghost story here relates to a piece of tragic history that supposedly occurred here in the mid 1900s.

A police officer caught a vehicle speeding on the road, and he pulled the car over near where the road dead-ends today. The officer got out of his car and walked up to the window of the speeder's vehicle to collect the driver's license and registration. Suddenly, a car came speeding by, and before anyone could react, the car smashed into the police officer, who was standing in the street next to the car he had pulled over. The officer was killed instantly.

ghost story

The ghost of the officer who was killed here in the 1950s supposedly haunts this road. Sometimes, if you park your car or drive near where the road ends today, you will get pulled over by a police officer in a 1950s-style police car. The officer will walk up to your window as if he is about to give you a ticket and will then suddenly disappear. The police car that was behind you vanishes at the same moment.

Another commonly told story about this part of Narrows Road involves a small boy on a bike. People will see a young boy, maybe five years old, riding his bike in the middle of the night. When he approaches them, they ask the boy what he is doing out by himself so late, but he will never answer. As soon as the witnesses glance away for a second, the boy vanishes without a trace.

visiting

The first time that I went to this site, I was pulled over by a police officer. Unfortunately, this one didn't disappear into thin air. According to this officer, there is a problem with teenagers using the secluded dead-end of Narrows Road as a place to make out or do drugs. As a result, police officers patrol the area regularly. While there is nothing illegal about going to the end of the road to look for ghosts, when I was stopped I was searched and my vehicle was searched. This can be an annoying inconvenience during a ghost hunt.

My advice is to keep your visits to this area short, and if you are stopped by the police, tell the truth about why you're there—I'm sure they've heard it before.

OXFORD MILFORD ROAD

Oxford Milford Road and Earhart Road, Oxford, OH 45056

directions

Take I-75 north to I-275 west. From I-275, take the Colerain Avenue exit (exit 33). Take Colerain Avenue/US-27 north, past Ross. Stay on this road for nearly eleven miles until it dead-ends in Millville. Turn left onto Millville Oxford Road and follow this road for ten miles. It will take you into Oxford. Just past the large sports fields on your right, turn left onto High Street. About a half-mile down High Street, turn right onto US-732. A little more than a mile down 732, turn right onto Somerville Road. Follow Somerville Road for two miles and then turn left onto Oxford Milford Road. Follow Oxford Milford Road for a little more than a mile until you get to the intersection with Earhart Road. You will need to turn your car around so you are facing south down Oxford Milford Road, away from Earhart. This is where the ghost resides.

history

According to legend, there were once two lovers who used to meet near this intersection. The girl was forbidden from seeing the boy by her parents since he had a rough reputation and drove a motorcycle, but this did not stop them from seeing each other. They worked out a system where the boy would wait down the street until the girl's parents were both asleep. Then she would signal the boy by flashing the porch lights three times. When he saw the signal he would ride up to the house on his motorcycle and off they'd go.

A couple different versions of the story exist as to what happened next. One version says that the girl's parents were up unusually late one night. The boy waited for the porch lights to flash but hours passed and nothing was happened. While he waited, he started drinking the beer he had brought. When the girl's parents finally went to bed and she flashed the lights, the boy was too drunk to safely drive his motorcycle to the house. He lost control and crashed and died.

Another version states that as he was driving up to the house he encountered a young child who was riding a small bicycle. He hit the child on the bicycle and crashed, killing the child and himself. Other versions of the story go on to say that the girl hung herself in her parents' barn after discovering that her boyfriend had been killed. We have researched this story through newspaper archives but have found nothing to verify it.

ghost story

The ghost story at this location is one of the most famous in southwest Ohio, and it is directly connected to the story of the boy and girl and their forbidden love affair. The story goes that if you sit in your car near the intersection of Earhart and Oxford Milford Road and face your car south down Oxford Milford Road, you may encounter this ghost. To summon it you need to flash your headlights three times. Flashing the lights supposedly simulates the girl flashing her porch lights three times to summon her boyfriend.

At this point, you are supposed to be able to see a single headlight coming down the road toward you—the boyfriend on his motorcycle. As the headlight gets nearer, it suddenly disappears, as if the motorcycle has crashed.

Some versions of the story include other elements, but all versions include the phantom headlight. Sometimes people will see what looks like red bicycle reflectors crossing the road before the headlight disappears. Other times people will see what look like flashing red emergency lights, as if emergency vehicles were working a crash scene.

visiting

One reason this ghostly location is so popular with ghosthunters is the ease of access. The road is open all night, of course, and the area is rather remote. The only other cars you are likely to see here late at night are driven by people who want to flash their lights looking for the ghost.

Another reason the ghost story is so popular is that this phenomenon actually happens quite often. Many people—skeptics and ghost enthusiasts alike—claim to have witnessed it. They will go to the site, not really expecting anything to happen, and they will be surprised when something actually does. Therefore, accessibility and frequency of sightings make this a great location to look for a ghost.

POND RUN ROAD

Pond Run Road, New Richmond, OH 45157

directions

Take I-471 south to I-275 east. Take I-275 to exit 71, the US-52/New Richmond exit. Take US-52 east toward New Richmond. Follow this road for about seven and a half miles. Pond Run Road will be on your left.

history

The history behind the ghost story on this road is perhaps as creepy as the ghost story itself. The story goes that the family who lived in a small house along Pond Run Road near the beginning of the twentieth century kept their son, a young man with some sort of mental disorder, chained in the basement of the house.

Of course, while the family lived there, no one from the area knew the son was chained. The secret was revealed one day when the house caught fire for some unknown reason. Both of the parents were killed in the blaze. When the townspeople were searching through the burned-out wreckage of the house they found the place in the basement where the parent had kept their son chained. All they found of the son, though, was one of his hands. Apparently, he somehow had severed his own hand in order to escape the chains. Some people suggest that once he escaped, he killed his parents and burned the house to the ground.

ghost story

Some people from nearby New Richmond claim that the story about Pond Run Road is the origin of the urban myth of the hook man. Years ago, Pond Run was a much more isolated place than it is today. From the 1950s all the way up through the 1980s, many teenagers from the area would go to the road, giving it a reputation as a lover's lane. Stories began to pop up, however, about a man who would stalk the woods near the road and attack these teenagers who were foolish enough to park nearby. They said that he had a hook for a hand. They said that he was the boy who had removed his own hand in order to kill his parents and burn down his house.

Today, there is much more development along this road so it is no longer a popular lover's lane. The hook man, though, apparently has not left. People will still report seeing a man with a hook for a hand walking through the area stalking vehicles. It doesn't seem to matter whether the cars are parked or if they are moving down the road. Many times the hook man will chase them. Most of the ghost stories about the hook man are the same as the urban myth. When people park their car along this road, a man with a hook for a hand will try to get into the car.

visiting

Some ghost stories sound a lot more like myth than like reality. The fact that they sound made up, however, doesn't make these places any less frightening at night.

Pond Run Road is open to the public at all times. It is a curvy road and it does get quite dark after the sun goes down, but as long as you drive carefully, it is completely safe. There are few places to pull to the side of the road to park, but the hook man is said to stalk both stationary and moving cars. If you find a place where you can stop your car safely, that may be your best bet for encountering the hook man (or at least for having a nerve-wrecking experience), but even if you can't find a place to stop, you'll still notice the road seems creepy. And when you get home, don't forget to check to see if there is a hook hanging from your car's door handle.

PRINCETON ROAD

2421 Princeton Road, Hamilton, OH 45011

directions

Take I-75 north to the Butler County Veteran's Highway (RT-129) toward Hamilton. When you reach the eastern end of Hamilton and the first couple of traffic lights, turn right onto Hampshire Drive. Hampshire Drive will dead-end into Princeton Road. Turn right onto Princeton, and Rose Hill Burial Park will be on your right. This is the beginning of the haunted section of the road.

history

According to the legends, a terrible car accident happened on this road. A young woman was excited about her upcoming prom. She had the perfect date and the perfect dress, and she couldn't wait for the event. When the day finally came, things immediately began going wrong. First, it started to rain. Then her date called her to say he would be unable to pick her up for the dance. Instead, he would have to meet her there. She wasn't willing to let these roadblocks ruin her night, however, and so she decided to drive herself and meet her date at the dance.

She got into her car, careful not to ruin her hair or her dress and began to drive. The fastest way route was to drive down Princeton Road near Rose Hill Burial Park and the Butler County Fairgrounds. A short distance past the cemetery, her car hit a puddle and she lost control. The crash killed her.

ghost story

A phantom hitchhiker haunts Princeton Road. Cars driving down the road will see a young girl in a prom dress hitchhiking along Princeton near Rose Hill Burial Park. Two different stories are told about her.

The first story involves the cars that actually stop to pick her up. The hitchhiker will get into the car and tell the driver where she wants to go. As they ride toward her destination the driver will be shocked to find that the young woman is gone. She somehow vanished from a moving car. The other stories involve the cars that don't stop to pick her up. After they pass her and head farther down Princeton Road, they will have a wreck.

Some people say that the ghost is the spirit of the girl who died on the way to her prom. Not even death is going to stop her from getting to that dance, so she hitchhikes. She is angry with those cars that don't stop to give her a ride, so some people say that she causes the accidents that result from people not picking her up. Others claim that she walks Princeton Road, warning passing motorists of danger in the road ahead.

visiting

The best way to drive when attempting to encounter this phantom hitchhiker is to begin your drive near the church on the western end of Princeton Road. Drive east down Princeton past Rose Hill Burial Park. According to the legends, the area just past the cemetery is where she was killed and where people encounter the apparition most frequently.

There is nothing stopping ghosthunters from driving up and down this road all night looking for the apparition. The road is quite straight and level and safe—which is unusual, since haunted roads tend to have hills and curves. If you see a young girl hitchhiking on the side of the road in her prom dress, it may be in your best interest to pick her up and take her wherever she wants to go. You wouldn't want to make her mad.

SPOOKY HOLLOW ROAD

Spooky Hollow Road, Cincinnati, OH 45242

directions

Take I-71 north to I-275 east. Take I-275 to the Loveland/Indian Hill exit (exit 57). Turn right onto Loveland-Madeira Road. Follow Loveland-Madeira Road for about two miles and turn right onto Spooky Hollow Road. You will be going up the hill that you are supposed to be going down, so when you get to the top of the hill, where you'll see a gray stone gate, turn around to coast down the haunted hill.

history

The history of this road is a ghost story in itself. In the area near what today is called Spooky Hollow Road, a man named Eli Dusky ran a sugar camp. Eli was really into ghosts and the occult, and one day he walked down to his homemade sugar vats and saw a group of small goblins dancing around them. Terrified, he ran all the way into town and told everyone what he had seen. Since his place was in a dark hollow and apparently was home to goblins there, the road was named Spooky Hollow.

In the 1940s through the early 1960s, people would often see a headless horseman riding down Spooky Hollow Road at night. Had they seen a ghost? Not really. The horseman was entirely explainable. There was a man who lived on Spooky Hollow Road who would dress up in a headless horseman costume and ride a horse up and down the road to get children in the mood for Halloween.

ghost story

The ghost story about this road involves the hill that you descend to get back to Loveland-Madeira Road. On top of the gray stone gate at the top of this hill, there was once a witch weathervane. Legend claims that if you are at the top of the hill at night near this gate, if you turn off your lights, put the car in neutral, and then descend the hill, a witch will run out in front of your car and cause you to wreck.

Another ghost story states that if you aim your car toward the gate and flash your lights three times, the gate will open up and a witch will beckon you inside.

visiting

First of all, DO NOT try to flash your lights at the gate. This is a person's house. The reason that the witch weathervane isn't there anymore is because too many people flashed their lights at the house, and the owners got fed up with it (and rightly so).

The other part of the ghost story, I'm not sure is even possible. The road is very curvy and very dark at night. You would have to know that road like the back of your hand to have any chance of making it down in neutral with your lights off. I can't imagine anyone ever making it all the way down with the lights off. In my opinion, if any cars did get in an accident with their lights off on this road, it wasn't the witch's fault—it was the idiot who tried to navigate down the hill in the pitch dark.

Since this location is so near two other locations in this book (Loveland-Madeira Road and Blome Road Bridge), it is definitely worth checking out. It is a creepy road, and it does send chills down your spine knowing that there is supposedly a witch that haunts the downhill curves. But I can't imagine anyone ever having actually turned off the lights off and coasted down this hill in neutral.

SECTION III

parks and trails

During the day, parks seem the opposite of creepy or scary. They're beautiful and fun. However, as the sun goes down, the beauty slowly succumbs to the darkness, and those things that went unnoticed during the day come to the forefront of one's mind. A swing that creaks as it moves in the wind. The sounds of unseen animals in the woods. And perhaps the remnants of someone long since passed away..

BUTLER COUNTY FAIRGROUNDS

1715 Fairgrove Avenue, Hamilton, OH 45011

directions

Take I-75 north to the Butler County Veteran's Highway (RT-129) toward Hamilton. Once you reach the eastern end of Hamilton and the first couple of traffic lights, turn right onto Fair Avenue. The fairgrounds will be the large grassy fields to your right.

history

The fairgrounds were set aside in 1856 to host the Butler County Fair. The fair rapidly grew and eventually became the largest agricultural fair in the state. As the event expanded, the fairgrounds expanded. A race track and grandstand were built, but the grandstand soon burnt to the ground in a mysterious fire. It was rebuilt with concrete and became the first concrete grandstand in the world. One year a man walked into the restrooms underneath the grandstands with a gun. He shot himself in the head and died in the restroom. Despite hours of research, we could not find evidence that this story is true or even has some basis in fact. It could be an urban myth or perhaps the family covered up the suicide to avoid embarrassment.

ghost story

Sometimes late at night, a mysterious man will walk out of the restrooms located underneath the concrete grandstands at the fairgrounds. He will roam around the area immediately surrounding the restrooms. Many times, witnesses will see this man from a distance. Those people who are unlucky enough to spot the man close up notice the massive gunshot wound in his head. People say that this is the ghost of the man who shot himself in the restroom.

This spirit is most often seen by workers who are cleaning up after the Butler County Fair has ended and the fairgrounds are all but empty. From time to time, however, people will see this figure while the fair is actually in operation.

visiting

It is unlikely that you will encounter this ghost if you are going to the fairgrounds to look for him. There are reports of people outside the fences seeing the ghost after the fair has been long closed, but most of the reports happen after dark during the time that the fair is running. Your best bet if you want to see this ghost is to go to the fair and stay until after dark. The best day for seeing the ghost is the last day of the fair.

The fair usually runs near the end of July and the beginning of August and it costs six dollars per person to get in. It is also possible to rent the fairgrounds during other times of the year, but the fee is quite expensive. If all else fails, you can always stand at the fence and look into the fairgrounds, hoping to see that strange figure walking around by the restrooms.

CAMP DENNISON

7650 Glendale Milford Road, Camp Dennison, OH 45111

directions

Take I-71 north to I-275 east. Take I-275 to the Wards Corner Road exit. Turn southwest off the exit and follow Wards Corner Road until you get to 126 (Center Street). Turn left onto 126/Center Street and then take your first right onto Glendale Milford Road. Follow Glendale Milford Road for about a mile and a half. On your right, you will pass the Waldschmidt House. To get to the grounds of the camp and the haunted bike trail, take a right onto Kugler Mill Road. The big field near the corner is the old camp.

history

Camp Dennison was built in 1861 as a Civil War training camp for Ohio soldiers. General George McClellan created the design for the camp, which was named after Ohio's Governor William Dennison. Problems erupted at the camp almost immediately. It opened in May, when it was unusually rainy and there were no permanent structures yet built. The soldiers had to build flimsy board structures to protect themselves from the elements. Beyond this inconvenience, the food was often inedible. The soldiers were forced to cook for themselves and many of them had no experience. At one point, the soldiers used the nearby creek as a bathroom. The drinking water for the camp was taken downstream from where they were relieving themselves.

Once the war got into full swing, the camp ran much more smoothly. They built hospitals on the site to help care for the soldiers who had been wounded in action. After the Battle of Shiloh, thousands of wounded Union soldiers poured into the hospitals at Camp Dennison. Many died there and were buried at a nearby cemetery.

ghost story

Several ghosts are said to haunt the grounds of Camp Dennison. The most famous ghost haunts the bike trail that runs where the old train tracks used to be when it was a training camp. People have reported that while walking down this bike trail, they have seen a man dressed in a Civil War uniform—a long blue coat and a blue soldier's hat—looking toward the camp. If this man is approached, he vanishes.

Also, people have seen buildings in the fields with dim lights in the windows when going by at night. When they drive past the same location the next day, the buildings have vanished. The rumor is that these buildings are remnants of the hospitals that used to sit in the fields.

Finally, the nearby cemetery is haunted. People will see dark figures walking through the cemetery at night, or they will hear screams or crying coming from the cemetery.

visiting

There are no legal or safety issues when visiting Camp Dennison at night. The open field and public bike trail have no signs or warnings about being there after dark. Out of courtesy, however, make sure you are quiet when visiting the site late at night. There are many houses in the area, and you do not want to wake up any of the locals.

The cemetery does close at night. If you enter after dark, you will be breaking the law. The ghosts that supposedly haunt the cemetery can be seen and heard from just outside of the gates, so it is not necessary to go into the closed cemetery.

CINCINNATI ZOO

3400 Vine Street, Cincinnati, OH 45220

directions

From I-75, take exit 6. Turn south onto West Mitchell Avenue. You'll see signs pointing you toward the zoo. About a quarter mile down the road, turn right onto Vine Street. The parking lot for the zoo will be on your right about a mile and a half down the road.

history

The Cincinnati Zoo was the second one built in the Western Hemisphere, after the zoo in Philadelphia, and it contains the Western Hemisphere's oldest standing zoo building, today's reptile house. From the time the zoo was built in 1875 until the present day, many animals have lived and died here. This zoo also housed the world's last passenger pigeon and the world's last Carolina Parakeet. After these animals died at the zoo, they were considered extinct.

ghost story

The ghost that haunts this location is that of a lion. That's right—a ghost lion walks the paths here at the zoo and will often watch passersby from the safety of the thick foliage that lines many of the paths. Witnesses claim to have been walking alone down a remote path and heard what sounded like the footfalls of a large lion behind them. Sometimes these witnesses have become so terrified that they broke into a run, hearing the sounds of the lion's footsteps keeping up with their every step. When they feel that the lion is about to strike, they turn to face their attacker only to see that there is nothing following them.

Other times, witnesses will see the glowing eyes of a lion looking out at them from the brush down a dark, out-of-the-way path. These witnesses slowly walk the other way, hoping the lion doesn't follow them.

visiting

The zoo is open to the public, of course, but it charges an admission fee, whether you're there to see the animals or to research the ghost stories. At the time of publication, the admission price was thirteen dollars. The zoo closes at six p.m. during the spring and summer and at five p.m. during fall and winter. If you want the added spookiness of being there at night, come to the annual Festival of Lights, which is held every November and December. At this event, the zoo is open until nine p.m. and so the place is open well past dark. The zoo also holds an event on weekends in October called "Hallzooween" where the themes and décor of the zoo are decorated for the Halloween season. This event is only open until five p.m., however, so you will have to leave the park before dark.

If you hope to find the ghost lion, linger on the more remote paths that weave through thick foliage. If you see the lion, it's all right to get scared. After all, this is a zoo, and it is entirely possible that the lion may not disappear before it attacks.

CONEY ISLAND

6201 Kellogg Avenue, Cincinnati, OH 45230

directions

Take I-471 south to I-275 east. Take I-275 to the Kellogg Avenue exit near the Ohio River on the east side of the city. Turn right (east) on Kellogg. Coney Island will be on your right.

history

Between 1500 and 2000 years ago, the Hopewell Indians frequented the land that is today Coney Island. There are still many mounds from mound-building Native American cultures in the surrounding area. Eventually, a European settler moved here and established an orchard. People moving through his orchard on the way to Cincinnati from the east would ask the owner if they could stop for a picnic on his land. He would always allow them to do it. Eventually the landowner built shelters and rides for his visitors.

In 1886, a company purchased the land and officially developed it as an amusement park. Perhaps the most famous owner of the park was a man named George Schott. He did much to make the park what it is today, including the construction of Moonlight Gardens, the dance floor and meeting area in the park. In 1935, Schott was attending an event at Moonlight Gardens when he suddenly had a heart attack and died.

Other tragedies have occurred at the park as well. A young boy was riding the Scrambler and was thrown off. A spinning car slammed into him and killed him. A woman was riding the merry-go-round when she suddenly suffered a dizzy spell. She fell from her horse, hit her head on the ground, and died. A man dove into Sunlight Pool to race his friends to the island at its center. His two friends made it to the island, but the man had hit his head on the bottom and drowned in the pool.

ghost story

Many ghost stories circulate about this park. Sometimes people will hear Indians chanting in the darkness, long after the park has closed. Other times people will witness strange fogs, which settle over the park—and only the park. Perhaps these fogs are giving the ghosts some privacy as they play.

The merry-go-round is haunted. People will hear commotion and screams coming from the ride even when there is no one nearby. Other times people will actually hear the merry-go-round music playing, even when the ride is shut down.

Sunlight Pool is haunted. When the pool is empty but filled with water, people will sometimes hear frantic splashing coming from the pool. Perhaps creepier, when the pool is empty and drained of water, people will still sometimes hear that frantic splashing.

Perhaps the most haunted spot in the park, however, is Moonlight Gardens. Many employees will not enter Moonlight Gardens at night. They claim that they feel uncomfortable and unwelcome there. Other times employees will see a man in the balcony area looking down at them. Sometimes this man is with a woman, but the general consensus is that this is the ghost of George Schott, haunting the area where he died so many years before.

visiting

To visit this haunted location, you will need to pay for admission. Tickets are about twelve dollars for either the Sunlight Pool or the rides, or you can get a pass for the whole park for twenty-two dollars. The park closes in September for the fall and winter and does not open up again until May. Perhaps the best time to visit the park to look for ghosts would be during the Fall-o-ween event held in October. The admission is slightly cheaper, and it gets dark earlier. Sunlight Pool is closed by this time too. Since it has been drained of water, you can stand outside the fence and listen for the ghostly sounds of splashing in the empty pool.

DELHI PARK

5125 Foley Road, Cincinnati, OH 45238

directions

Take US-50 west from downtown Cincinnati. Turn right on Fairbanks Road and go up the hill to Delhi Pike. Turn left on Delhi Pike. A couple miles up the hill you will see a McDonald's on your right. The driveway for the park is just before the McDonald's driveway.

history

The lake, which is now a part of the park, was once part of a separate property next to the park called the Clearview Tavern. According to legend, several people have drowned in the lake over the years. One story involves a man who was drowning in the lake and a friend dove in to attempt to save him. When the friend reached the drowning man, they were caught in a strong undertow and they both drowned. While I could not find historic proof of this story, I did find evidence that another man killed himself in the lake one night in the 1990s.

There does seem to be some kind of force at the lake that tries to suck people under the water. There have been several documented instances where people were pulled under and were narrowly saved before drowning.

ghost story

If you enter the park after dark, the ghosts come out. Many witnesses have encountered the apparitions of two men who appear as shadowy figures and often approach both pedestrians and vehicles entering the park after dark. Their approach is menacing, prompting the witnesses who encounter them to head toward the exits. The two shadowy figures will follow witnesses until they leave the park, at which point the apparitions vanish.

Many people attribute the existence of these apparitions to the two men who drowned in Clearview Lake, close to the entrance of the park.

visiting

The park does not close until eleven p.m., providing a span of a few hours after the sun has set when you can enter legally. Because the shadowy figures tend to show up when there is one person or a small group in the park at night, you'll want to avoid the sporting events or other large gatherings that sometimes take place here after dusk. To test the legend of the shadowy figures, you can either walk or drive through the park. The shadowy figures have been known to approach both cars and pedestrians. Most of the time, the figures originate in the fenced-in area directly across the road from Clearview Lake. A swing set used to stand here and the figures often were seen near it. Though the swing set is gone, the spot remains a favorite place for the figures to appear.

DUNHAM PARK

4320 Guerley Road, Cincinnati, OH 45238

directions

Take I-75 north to the Harrison Avenue exit. Follow the signs to Queen City Avenue. Take Queen City Avenue up the hill until you get to Sunset Avenue. Turn left on Sunset and follow Sunset until the road curves at Guerley Road. Turn right at Guerley. Your first right on Guerley is the entrance to the park.

history

Before it was a park, this area was known as the Guerley Farm. In 1897, University Hospital began transferring tuberculosis patients to this farm until, in 1912, the Cincinnati Tubercular Hospital opened here. At that time most people afflicted with tuberculosis eventually died from it, meaning that thousands of patients died on these grounds. In 1927 the facility was renamed the Hamilton County Tuberculosis Sanatorium and then in 1945 the name changed to Dunham Hospital, after Dr. Henry Dunham, an important doctor at the facility from 1909 to 1940.

On the west side of the facility sat the theater and the laundry buildings, which are the only ones that survived after the area was turned into a park in 1973. The theater building is still used as a performing arts center while the laundry building is used as a garage for maintenance vehicles.

The main hospital building stood in the center of the park. With two wings around a central tower, it stood five stories tall and there were balconies where the patients would spend most of their time. In those days it was thought that winter air would help cure the disease. Also, patients could see visitors from the balconies without exposing visitors to infection. When the hospital was shut down, the main building was destroyed, though the parking lot is still there.

Two other buildings occupied the hill on the east side of the complex—a white house, which still stands, that was used as the home of the head doctor as well as a building that housed children whose parents were afflicted by the disease. That building was replaced by one that is used by the Cincinnati Recreation Commission as a children's theater and entertainment area.

ghost story

Every building here has its own ghost or two, and the park itself is also haunted. The doors throughout the old theater building on the west side of the park will slam shut, and figures will be seen in the hallways, ducking into rooms and then disappearing. Also, people will hear coughing when no one else is there.

In the garage, people will see women in white nurse's uniforms walk into the building and then disappear. Figures are seen walking around outside the doctor's house. They disappear when approached. Where the children's building used to be, people will see ghost children or hear children's voices when they are in or near the building—especially near the back of the building or the yard in the back.

There is also a lot of activity in the center of the park where the main hospital building used to stand. People will hear coughing and moaning here even when there is no one else nearby. At night, people will see figures walking aimlessly throughout the area. When these figures are approached, either they vanish or they continue to walk aimlessly, not taking any notice of anyone or anything.

visiting

The grounds are easy to visit, but it is next to impossible to enter the buildings, which are closed to everyone except those who work in them. But with the exception of the theater building and the children's building, most of the hauntings occur outside. The park is open to the public all day, and it doesn't close until ten o'clock. The best time to go with the best chance of witnessing the ghosts is after dark but before ten. There are rarely any people in the park during this time so you probably will have the entire area to yourself.

EDEN PARK

1198 Eden Park Drive, Cincinnati, OH 45202

directions

Take I-71 north from downtown. The first exit after the tunnel is Eden Park Drive, and it's on the left side of the highway. Take that exit and then turn right at the end of the ramp. This will take you into Eden Park. At the first fork in the road inside the park, go left. The haunted gazebo will be on your right next to the reflecting pool. You'll find parking across the street from the gazebo.

history

George Remus was the most prolific bootlegger in Cincinnati during prohibition in the 1920s, and he made quite a bit of money doing it. Eventually, however, he went to prison for his illegal activities, serving time in a federal prison in Atlanta, Georgia. While in prison, he befriended a fellow inmate named Frank Dodge and told him all about his operations and his money and how he trusted his wife, Imogene, enough to give her complete power of attorney over his assets.

Unfortunately for George, Frank Dodge was actually an undercover FBI agent who was investigating the warden of the prison, so when Dodge learned about Remus's operation, he left the prison, quit the FBI, and went to Cincinnati. While in Cincinnati, he seduced Imogene, and they fell in love and began taking all of George's assets. At one point, they tried to pay a hitman to kill George, but their plot failed.

When George was released from prison, he was furious and immediately filed for divorce. Imogene was more that happy to oblige his request. The divorce got messy and had to go to court, so to mark the occasion, Imogene wore a black dress to the courthouse. On the way to the courthouse, George saw Imogene's taxi and ran her off the road at the gazebo in Eden Park. They both jumped out of their vehicles and started arguing. At the height of the argument, George took out a pistol and shot Imogene dead just outside of the gazebo.

George was arrested and tried for the murder of his wife, but he was able to get off by pleading temporary insanity. He did not spend a single day in prison for the murder.

ghost story

Only one ghost haunts the gazebo at Eden Park. It is the ghost of a woman in a black dress, probably the ghost of Imogene Remus. People have seen this woman in black standing inside the gazebo. Often she is seen gazing across the reflecting pool. Onlookers always sense that something is wrong with her. When they approach, she vanishes. The ghost will usually appear at dusk or late at night.

visiting

During the day, this location is easy to visit. There is a parking lot just across the street from the gazebo, and the area is always open during daylight hours. Unfortunately, the area closes at dark, which is when the ghost is said to appear. This leaves a few choices. First, you could stay until dusk when the ghost will sometimes appear. Second, the area is not closed to vehicular traffic, so you could drive by the gazebo late at night in an attempt to see the ghost. To me, the difference between going at dusk versus at night doesn't seem worth the trespassing charges that may be leveled against you. I have also heard that paranormal investigation groups have been given special permission to investigate the area after dark. It cannot hurt to contact Cincinnati Parks to ask for permission.

HARBIN PARK

1300 Hunter Road, Fairfield, OH 45014

directions

Take I-75 north to I-275 west. Take I-275 to the Hamilton Avenue/OH-127 exit. Take Hamilton Avenue north for about two and a half miles. Then turn left onto Hunter Road, which will take you directly into the park after about a half-mile. Once inside the park, turn left at the first fork in the road. This will take you down to a parking lot near the Frisbee golf course. The haunted area of the park is near the water tower, which should be directly in front of you.

history

The historic origins of the ghost that haunts the park in Fairfield can be traced back to an accident that happened at the water tower near the Frisbee golf course. A group of teenagers decided to jump the fence by the water tower. Several of them started putting graffiti on a small maintenance building adjacent to the tower, but one teen decided that he would impress his friends by climbing up the tower to vandalize the top. When he got to the top of the tower, he slipped and fell all the way down to his death.

Today, the water tower still stands, and graffiti is still on the small maintenance building beside it. The fence around it is taller and more difficult to scale than it was when the vandal fell from the tower. The park itself is a popular place to play Frisbee golf and also has many popular bike trails. Since the boy fell from the tower, there have been no other fatalities at the park.

ghost story

The ghost of the boy who fell from the water tower resides here at this park. People report hearing screams coming from the area near the water tower. These screams are usually heard on clear nights. When people hear the screams and investigate, they find that there is no one there.

Sometimes, the ghost at Harbin Park is actually seen. People will see a teenage boy walking around by the gazebo between the Frisbee golf course and the water tower at dusk by himself. They don't pay much attention to the boy until they notice that suddenly he is no longer there, and the immediate area offers no place he could hide. He has simply vanished.

visiting

The park closes at night so it is not easy to gain access legally after dark. During the summer, the park closes at 9:30 p.m., which sometimes allows for a bit of searching after dark, but during the fall and winter it usually closes right around dusk.

Although there are times when people will witness the apparition and screams during the day, the ghostly sounds and figures are seen and heard most often after dark, so this ghost could be tricky to find. Your best bet is to try to stay in the park as long as you can without violating the posted hours.

HERITAGE VILLAGE

11450 Lebanon Pike, Sharonville, OH 45241

directions

Take I-75 north to I-275 east. Take I-275 to exit 46, Mason/Sharonville. Turn toward Sharonville—south on Lebanon Road. Less than a mile down the road, turn left into Sharon Woods Park at a road called Buckeye Falls Drive. This road becomes South Meadoe Drive. Follow the road until you see the signs for the Heritage Village. Parking is across the street from the actual village.

history

This village was set up in Sharon Woods to show what life was like in the days when European-Americans first began to settle in Southwest Ohio. While the village itself is rather new, the buildings themselves are all quite old and were moved from their original locations in the areas surrounding Sharon Woods.

The Hayner House was an old farmhouse built in the mid-1800s. It was originally located near Lebanon and was moved to Heritage Village in 1967. The Elk Lick House was constructed in the early 1800s, perhaps as early as 1818, and was expanded upon throughout the nineteenth century. The size and design of the house suggest that it was used by a wealthy landowner from the area. The house was saved from demolition in 1969 and moved to Heritage Village. The third haunted building in the village, the Vorhes House, was built between 1820 and 1830 and is not as lavish as the previous two. It was moved to Heritage Village from Blue Ash.

A generally accepted theory about ghosts suggests that any sort of restoration work kicks up a lot of paranormal activity. Imagine what moving an entire building might do.

ghost story

Most of the ghostly encounters take place at the Hayner House, where a vast array of paranormal phenomena has been reported. The sounds of a party—laughing, talking, and the clinking of glasses—can be heard coming from the building, even when it is empty. While the phantom parties may be the most elaborate haunting within the building, there are many more strange stories that bolster the haunted reputation of the place. People will often feel uncomfortable when they enter the house alone. They feel chills down their spines and will even sometimes feel physically cold sensations throughout the house—especially the upstairs. Lights flicker on and off by themselves, and items will vanish only to reappear at other strange places.

The Vorhes House and the Elklick House are also supposedly home to some spirits. In these houses, people who enter alone often feel a sense of dread. They feel unwelcome, as if some unseen being or force wants them out of the house. Also, doors will close by themselves and cold spots are often felt within these houses.

visiting

Heritage Village is open during weekends in April and is open during the summer until September. It closes at five every day and is closed on Mondays. Admission is five dollars for adults and three dollars for children under eleven.

Beyond these regular hours, the village hosts special events throughout the year. On weekends in October they have a haunted attraction where the village is given a more sinister and scary theme. It is open from six to ten p.m. and the admission is ten dollars for adults, but it allows for the opportunity to explore the village during the creepier evening hours. The village also opens in December when it is decorated for Christmas. During the times when the village is open, the buildings are open to the public.

KINGS ISLAND

Kings Island Drive, Mason, OH 45050

directions

Take I-71 north to the Western Row Road exit (exit 24). If you continue to go straight at the end of the exit ramp, the road changes its name to Kings Island Drive. Follow Kings Island Drive for about a quarter mile. Kings Island will be on your right.

history

Construction on this iconic amusement park just north of Cincinnati began in 1970, and it opened to the public in 1972. Kings Island immediately became successful, and it is still expanding and becoming more popular to this day.

Through the years, however, tragic accidents have happened here. According to legend, one occurred at the Eiffel Tower exhibit. On his high school graduation night (many people mark the date as May 13), a young man climbed the fence that separated the elevator from the public at the bottom of the tower. He then decided he would climb up the tower's stairs. As the elevator began to rise up the shaft, he tried to jump on and ride it to the top, but as he jumped, he became tangled in the cables and was cut in half.

In June of 1990, a woman dropped something into a scenic pond so she waded into the water to retrieve it. Some electrical wiring in the pond was poorly insulated and completely electrified the water. She was electrocuted and died. When a passing employee saw her in the water, he jumped in to save her and was electrocuted and died. A woman seated upside down on a ride called the Flight Commander saw the emergency vehicles racing to the electrified pond. To get a better view she squirmed in her seat and fell from the ride to her death.

There are rumors of other fatal accidents, such as a fatality at the Beast rollercoaster and one on the ride known as the Octopus.

ghost story

Many ghosts supposedly walk the grounds of Kings Island. One is that of a small girl seen most often near the Boomerang Bay Water Park area. She is always wearing a blue dress and vanishes when approached. Sometimes she jumps in front of the tram that goes from the main park to the water park but then will vanish. Supposedly, the little girl was buried in the nearby cemetery located between the campground and the parking lot.

Probably the most famous ghost is known as Tower Johnny—the ghost of the high school student who died at the Eiffel Tower. He is most often spotted at the tower, climbing the stairs beside the elevator or on the observation deck. He also is seen near the Beast rollercoaster, where, according to legend, the cables that cut him in half were eventually removed from the elevator and tossed into a heap.

Many other ghosts haunt the park. Sometimes people will see strange figures mysteriously vanish near the Beast. The ride known as the Monster is haunted by a strange figure who walks near the ride and keeps to the shadows before disappearing. The White Water Canyon ride is haunted by a ghost that employees call Woody. He likes to throw rocks at the back of a tower where employees operate and monitor the ride.

visiting

This location can only be visited during business hours, but the park is open after dark, so it is possible to walk around while it is at its creepiest. Unfortunately, the park is only open for about half of the year. After Halloween, the park closes until May. Also, access to the park can be expensive. You'll get your money's worth, but at the publication of this book, admission is $44.95 for adults and $29.95 for children. If you go to the park with the intention of searching for ghosts, it's best to go on a rainy weekday, when crowds are smaller than usual.

OLD MIAMIVILLE TRAIN TRACKS

Center Street and Glendale Milford Road, Miamiville,
OH 45147

directions

Take I-71 north to I-275 east. Take I-275 to the Loveland/Indian Hill exit. Turn right
onto Loveland Madeira Road, away from Loveland. Follow Loveland Madeira Road
until you reach the intersection with SR-126. Turn left onto 126. At one point in
the road, 126 makes a 90-degree turn at a cemetery. Just past this point, a bike trail
crosses 126. Train tracks once ran along the Little Miami River at this point, and this
is where the trainman is often seen.

history

While this area is lined now by concrete walking paths, through much of the twentieth
century there were train tracks that ran through Miamiville carrying anything from
war supplies to soldiers to passengers.

During the Civil War, this stretch of track was important to the Union cause. Troops and supplies from the northeast would travel through Miamiville on the way to Camp Dennison, the Union army training camp. In 1863, a group of Confederate cavalrymen known as Morgan's Raiders moved north into Ohio, and they attempted to disrupt the Union war effort. One of their attempts took place at the train tracks in Miamiville.

Morgan's Raiders piled a barricade of rail ties onto the tracks just past a turn in Miamiville. A man named Cornelius Conway was the engineer on the oncoming train. By the time he was able to see the barricade, it was too late. The train hit the barricade and derailed. Cornelius was killed.

ghost story

People will see Cornelius walking along where the old railroad tracks used to be. They will see a man in an old trainman uniform walking down the tracks carrying an old lantern. This apparition was first reported in the late 1800s, and stories circulated throughout Miamiville that the ghost of Cornelius Conway continued to haunt the tracks where he was killed. While the trains still ran along the tracks, engineers would see a man with a lantern walking down the tracks and would be forced to stop their trains. When they got out to investigate, they couldn't find anyone. The man on the tracks had vanished.

The stories still exist, and people still report seeing him to this day. People suggest that Cornelius isn't a malevolent spirit. He walks where the tracks once were to warn passersby of danger ahead.

visiting

The bike trail where the ghost is seen is quite accessible, even at night. There are places to park along 126 near the trail, and there are no signs suggesting that the area is closed after dark. It is possible that if you were walking down the trail in the middle of the night with a flashlight, a passing law enforcement officer may stop and ask what you are doing. I don't think it would cause a problem if you told him the truth—everyone in Miamiville knows about old Cornelius.

RAPID RUN PARK

4450 Rapid Run Parkway, Cincinnati, OH 45238

directions

Take I-75 north to the Harrison Avenue exit. Follow the exit toward Queen City Avenue. Follow Queen City Avenue up the hill until you get to a traffic light at Sunset Avenue. Turn left onto Sunset. Sunset will eventually change its name to Rapid Run. The park will be on your right. From the parking lot, simply climb the hill to its crest. The haunted swing set is there at the top of the hill.

history

Rapid Run Park was built in the late 1930s and early 1940s. Perhaps the most recognizable features in the park are the pavilion and the reflecting pond that the pavilion overlooks. The pavilion was built in 1941. I was unable to locate records of any tragedies that have occurred here, which makes the origins of the ghosts more mysterious since there doesn't seem to be any reason that ghosts would walk this park.

ghost story

Two sections of this park are supposedly haunted. The first is the swing set that sits at the top of the hill. On many different occasions, people have seen a little boy on the swing late at night. He disappears without a trace. Sometimes this boy is seen by an entire group of people at the same time. Other times, a single swing will begin to move back and forth for no reason; the other swings in the structure remain completely still.

People will also encounter ghosts at both the baseball fields and the nearby shelter. Witnesses will encounter figures that walk through these areas and then vanish.

visiting

Unfortunately, this park closes at ten p.m. During the winter months, however, you'll have plenty of time to legally enter the park after dark if you are interested in searching for these ghosts. Since the sightings seem to occur only at night, you will want to enter the park after the sun has set.

It is a bad idea to attempt to go to the park after it officially closes. The only parking is right next to Rapid Run, and police officers drive that road frequently. If they see a car in a closed park, they will most likely search for the trespassers. It is easier to visit the park after the sun goes down but before it closes for the night.

SLEEPER'S HILL SEDAMSVILLE WOODS

Corner of US-50 and Fairbanks Road, Cincinnati, OH 45204

directions

From downtown Cincinnati, take US-50 west. Just past the first gas station you see, you'll find Fairbanks Road. Turn right. There is a park at the corner of Fairbanks and Route 50. Sleeper's Hill is the wooded hill directly behind this park.

history

In the 1950s a man whose last name was Sleeper lived in a farmhouse up on this hill. He was a hermit, and he hated when anyone trespassed onto his property. He would take out his gun and chase them away. Other times he would chase people away with an axe, or he would even sometimes set his bull loose to chase the trespassers away. Parents warned their children to stay away from that hill.

Eventually Old Man Sleeper hung himself in his barn that sat at the top of the hill. Today the foundations of the old farmhouse are still visible up at the top of the hill. There are several private residences up there.

ghost story

The most famous ghost story about these woods on the hill is that people who trespass at night are chased away by a man with a bloody axe, perhaps the ghost of Old Man Sleeper, still protecting his property despite the fact that he is dead.

Other times, people will see an old man walking through the woods in the middle of the night. The man never acknowledges anyone, just simply walks by, appearing from a tree line and disappearing into the opposite tree line. Again, perhaps this is the ghost of Old Man Sleeper, forever wandering his property.

visiting

There has never been a report of someone being killed by the man with the bloody axe. At the same time, if the man with the bloody axe actually did catch someone, would anyone be able to tell the story?

This location is a tricky one to visit. Private homes have been built up there, and some of the owners have large dogs and would likely not appreciate you walking through their property in the dead of night. If you insist on walking these haunted woods at night, stay as far away as possible from anyone's home.

Whenever I have visited this site, I have always gone during the day. I went to the park and walked up into the forest behind the park to get a sense of the terrain. During daylight is the easiest time to access these woods, but if you can somehow safely find your way in at night, I'm sure that it would be much creepier.

SECTION IV

museums and theaters

It is considered good luck to have a ghost in your theater. Those at the theater assume that maybe the shows are so good that even those who have 'shuffled off this mortal coil' are intent upon seeing the performance. The more likely reason for these ghosts, though, may be an inherent dedication to the theater from those who have worked or visited there. After all, the show must go on.

I feel that museums should share the same superstition that it is lucky to have a ghost. After all, museums are essentially monuments to something, and this something is most often the past. What better way to exhibit the past than to house the spirit of someone who perhaps lived it?

CINCINNATI ART MUSEUM
953 Eden Park Drive, Cincinnati, OH 45202

directions
Take I-71 north from downtown to the first exit on the left after the tunnel—the Eden Park Drive exit. Turn right at the stoplight at the end of the exit ramp. This road will take you directly into Eden Park. At the first fork in the road, go right. You will go up a sharply curving hill. Near the top of the hill you'll see the sign for the Cincinnati Art Museum on your right.

history
Built in 1881, the Cincinnati Art Museum was the first art museum in North America west of the Appalachian Mountains. It has undergone many renovations and expansions, which have made it a very interesting building. The extensions and wings that have been added create a sense that the museum is a conglomeration of different buildings that happen to connect into a single structure. In 1976, the museum purchased the sarcophagus around which most of the ghost stories circulate.

ghost story
A sarcophagus in the Egyptian art section holds the most famous ghost of the museum. People will see black mists rise up from this sarcophagus and disappear into

the ceiling above. The room directly above the sarcophagus is a storage closet in which security guards used to sneak a nap. Once a security guard awoke in the room to find a menacing head floating directly in front of him. He tried to flee, but the floating head managed to keep itself between him and the door. This terrifying ordeal continued for quite some time before the guard was finally able to escape the room.

Other employees have seen what looks like the shadows of someone who has hung him or herself in the main room with the staircase. This room looks all the way up to the third floor, where a balcony looks all the way down to the first floor. The rumor among the employees is that there was a man who many years back hung himself from that balcony, and these shadows are the spectral remnants of that suicide.

visiting

The ghosts here usually appear during business hours, especially near closing time, so it is very easy to visit this place in an attempt to find the ghosts. Admission is free, but they do charge for parking, so unless you want to walk all the way from the lot at the bottom of the hill to the entrance, you will have to pay a small fee to visit the museum. The sarcophagus and main hall are open to the public but the storage closet where the unfortunate security guard encountered the floating head is off limits.

If you take a camera, make sure you stop by the front desk and grab a photography permit. They are free, but you need the official rules if you want to take pictures within the museum.

CINCINNATI MUSEUM CENTER

1301 Western Avenue, Cincinnati, OH 45203

directions

Take I-75 north to the Ezzard Charles Drive exit near downtown. Follow Ezzard Charles drive to the west (left). The Union Terminal is a giant half-dome structure at the western end of the road. You can't miss it.

history

Seven different train companies originally had their own stations throughout Cincinnati. This situation quickly became unfeasible, as people would have to travel across the city in order to catch a connecting train at a different company's station. To correct the problem, the city decided to bring all the stations together in one large train terminal located just outside of the downtown area. In 1931, the structure was completed, and life for travelers became much simpler. During World War II, Union Terminal was particularly busy due to the many soldiers who were shipping out to go to war. Many people saw their loved ones for the last time here as the soldiers went off to Europe never to return home.

With the advent of the Interstate Highway System and passenger plane travel, passenger trains were used less and less frequently until, in 1972, the last train company pulled out of the terminal. By the early 1980s, in an attempt to save the beautiful architectural masterpiece, Union Terminal was turned into a mall with restaurants, stores, and a bowling alley. This concept, however, was not successful and once again the terminal was closed.

For a while, the terminal sat empty and abandoned, but in the late 1980s the city decided to turn it into the museum center, which comprises the Cincinnati History Museum, the Museum of Natural History and Science, the Duke Energy Children's Museum, and the Omnimax Theater. Before the center opened in 1990, contractors worked on the building during the day, and a staff of security guards watched it at night. On September 6, 1989, a guard named Shirley Baker was watching the building when three men broke in. They overpowered her and kicked her to death.

ghost story

The ghost that is reported most often in the building is Shirley Baker. Many employees say they have either seen Shirley or felt her presence, especially when they are alone in certain parts of the building. Shirley appears as a female security guard who sometimes vanishes into thin air. Other times employees will see her and ask the other security guards about the new female officer who doesn't talk much. The staff will say that there is no new female security guard. They know that the witness has just seen Shirley.

Other ghosts haunt the building as well. On the landing that was used for loading and unloading passengers back in the days when the building was an active train terminal, people will hear sobbing and all kinds of other commotion even when the area is empty. Perhaps these are the ghosts of the people who saw their loved ones here for the last time before they were shipped off to war, never to return.

The Cincinnati History Museum, which is now located at the terminal, is also haunted. People will see a figure sitting inside of the plane that hangs from the ceiling. When these witnesses see the plane again on their way out, they notice that the cockpit is empty. When they ask about it, the employees tell them that there has never been a mannequin or person in that plane.

visiting

You have to visit during regular business hours, which you can find at the center's Web site, www.cincymuseum.org. You can enter the building itself for free, and the train-loading area is accessible without paying a fee, but you need to pay admission if you want to enter the Cincinnati History Museum or the Natural History Museum. There is the ghost in the plane in the Cincinnati History Museum, but Shirley has been seen most often in the Natural History Museum during the lonelier times of the day before the big crowds move in. Admission to these museums is eight dollars each, or you can pay twelve dollars if you want to go to both museums. They are open from ten a.m. to five p.m. every day but Sunday, when the center is open from eleven a.m. to six p.m. You may also have to pay the entry fee in order to visit certain locations in the building. There is a parking lot just outside the building where you can park your car for five dollars.

GLENDOWER MANSION

105 Cincinnati Avenue, Lebanon, OH 45036

directions

Take I-71 north to exit 28, OH-48/OH-48 North/Lebanon/Lebanon Raceway. Take the OH-123 ramp toward OH-48/US-42 S/Lebanon. Turn left onto OH-123/East Main Street and follow that road for about a mile. Turn left onto South Broadway/US-42. Turn right onto Cincinnati Avenue just before a small bridge. The house will be on your left at the top of the hill. The driveway is just past the businesses located at the corner.

history

Glendower was built in the 1840s and then was expanded during the time immediately following the Civil War. It was one of the largest mansions in Lebanon and was a centerpiece of the social scene of high society in the area. The original owner of Glendower was a man named John Milton Williams, a politician who worked on the constitution for the state of Ohio.

Throughout the years of its existence, many people lived at the house or visited it. Many parties took place there. Today, the mansion is owned by the Warren County Historical Society. Several times during the year, the building is open to the public for tours.

ghost story

Strange things seem to happen quite often within the walls of this large mansion. People will hear the sounds of a raging fire in the fireplace despite the fact that there is not a fire burning. People will sometimes also see strange lights that will typically climb the stairs and will not have any discernible source. Many people claim that when they approach the front door of the mansion, they will hear the sounds of a party inside. Thinking that the building was empty, they approach with a degree of confusion and caution. When they open the front door, they find that, in fact, the building is empty and silent. The sounds of the party disappear.

Other times, people hear what sounds like music coming from the front parlor. This will often happen when people are in other sections of the house. When they approach the front parlor to investigate, the music disappears.

visiting

At times throughout the year, the building is open to the public for tours. Unfortunately, it is difficult to determine what the hours are from year to year. You may want to call the Glendower Mansion at 513-932-1817 to check on hours of operation. The building is open Tuesday through Saturday from ten to four and costs five dollars for admission.

It's difficult to tell if these same hours will apply in subsequent years, but the only opportunity you will likely have to encounter the ghosts here at Glendower will be while the building is open to the public. When it is closed, a gate at the top of the long driveway at Cincinnati Avenue is closed and the house is impossible to access.

LOVELAND CASTLE

12025 Shore Road, Loveland, OH 45140

directions

Take I-71 north from Cincinnati to the Mason Montgomery Road exit (exit 19) toward Fields Ertel Road. Turn left on Mason Road. Turn right on Fields Ertel Road and follow it for about two and a half miles. When you get to Rich Road, turn right. Then turn left on Mulberry Street. Less than a half a mile down Mulberry Street, turn right onto Shore Road. The castle is right there.

history

It may seem hard to believe by looking at this beautiful castle, but the entire building was built by hand by one man. Harry Andrews went to Europe during WWI, and while he was there, he saw a lot of genuine European castles. When he returned to the states, his fiancé had left him for another man because the army had mistakenly reported to her that Harry Andrews had died at Fort Dix of disease. With his fiancé gone, Harry took charge of a group of Boy Scouts to help occupy his time. He named his troop the Knights of the Golden Trail.

Harry built a camp for the Knights of the Golden Trail next to the Little Miami River, but this camp would be destroyed each year by weather. He decided to build the camp from stones he recovered from the riverbed. After constructing a couple small rooms, he decided to expand. After all, his Knights needed a castle. He started building the castle but soon ran out of stones. He eventually created his own stones by filling empty milk cartons with concrete. Soon he and his Knights had a respectable castle.

Once, Harry and some of his Knights heard an explosion down by the river. They found a small cave where a woman had been operating a moonshine still that exploded, killing her.

Harry lived out the rest of his life in the castle. In 1981, he was burning garbage on his front lawn, and when he attempted to stomp out the remainder of the flames, his pants caught fire and he died from the wounds he sustained.

ghost story

Several ghost stories are told time and again about this castle. Inside the castle, people will often see shadows and hear footsteps moving through the rooms and the corridors. When they look to see who is there, they find no one. People claim that this is the ghost of Harry Andrews. Since he spent his life here in the building he built with his own hands and he died here in a tragic accident, he has every reason to haunt these halls.

Another story concerns a woman in white who will approach people at the castle and then mysteriously disappear. People claim that this is the ghost of the woman who died in the moonshine still explosion at the river near the castle.

Other ghost stories don't really seem to have an origin. Once, the bathroom door slammed closed several times for no reason. Someone thought that the ghost was trying to tell them something, and sure enough, the septic tank was about to overflow. The ghost saved the building thousands of dollars in repairs. Another ghost supposedly haunts the willow tree on the grounds. A creature shaped like an egg will float around near the willow tree. Other times, visitors will get electric shocks when they are misbehaving.

Harry Andrews witnessed a ghost himself while he was still alive. In the middle of the night, he would often hear a knocking at his front door. When he checked, he saw no sign that anyone had been there. One night after a heavy snow, he heard the knocks again. When he answered the door, he saw no one, and there were no tracks in the snow.

visiting

The Loveland Castle is very open about their ghosts, and all the employees that we have talked to were more than happy to discuss the ghosts. Admission to the castle is only three dollars. It is open seven days a week throughout the summer from eleven till five. From October to March, the castle is only open on weekends, from eleven till five, unless there is bad weather in which case it's closed.

The castle also holds a "haunted house" attraction during October weekend nights. The admission price as of this writing is eight dollars.

There is also the option of renting the entire building for some ghosthunting fun. Contact the castle for details. My impression is that you can rent the building overnight for $350. You can bring your ghosthunting equipment. Contact the staff to determine the cost as well as the number of people you can bring with you. This option is not available during October.

MT. HEALTHY MUSEUM

1546 McMakin Avenue, Mt. Healthy, OH 45231

directions

Take I-75 north from Cincinnati to I-275 west. Take I-275 to the SR-127/Hamilton Avenue exit. Take Hamilton Avenue south toward Mt. Healthy. When you get into the business district of Mt. Healthy, turn left at McMakin Avenue. About two blocks down the road, you will see the Mt. Healthy Museum on your left.

history

The museum is run by the local historical society, and it consists of two buildings. The main building was once the Free Meeting House in Mt. Healthy. Built in 1825, it was used to host community events. Since there were no churches in the town in 1825, many congregations would meet at the building. Reservations were granted on a first-come, first-served basis, and when disagreements arose between groups about who had rights at a particular time, the dispute was settled by a roll of the dice. Eventually, the building was set for demolition, but the Mt. Healthy Historic Society purchased it and moved it to the current location on McMakin Avenue.

The second building in the museum was once a tollhouse along Hamilton Avenue when Hamilton Avenue used to be a toll road. This building was also moved down the street from its original location and currently sits beside the Free Meeting House on McMakin Avenue.

ghost story

Several strange things are reported at these buildings. Most of the activity takes place within the Free Meeting House. People have seen strange shadows moving throughout the building. Sometimes people feel incredibly uncomfortable there, as if they are being watched, or they will get an eerie chill that climbs up their spine.

Perhaps the most frequently reported activity occurs when the place is empty. Members of the historical society will remember leaving something in the building a certain way the night before, but when they return the next day, things have been rearranged though no one has entered in the meantime.

visiting

The museum is run by volunteers who do not keep regular hours. You need to call 513-521-8168 and set up a tour. This situation is a mixed blessing. On the one hand, it makes it more difficult to access the building, but it also increases your chances of being alone while you're there.

Also, paranormal groups have been allowed access to the building. If you are part of a paranormal group, it may be worth your while to speak with the historical society about investigating the building. When I spoke to them about their history and ghosts, they were very open to the idea and were excited that their ghosts have sparked some interest in the history of their town.

PROMONTHOUSE
906 Main Street, Milford, OH 45150

directions
Take I-71 north to I-275 east. From I-275, take exit 57, Blanchester/Milford. Turn southwest onto OH-28 and follow that road for almost a mile. The house will be up the hill on your left.

history
Promont means "house on a hill." It was built in 1867 by a man named William McGrue, but the house gained its local fame through a later owner named John M. Pattison, who owned the house from 1879 until the early twentieth century. Pattison was the forty-third governor of Ohio, and he raised his family here.

The house is a beautiful example of Italianate Victorian architecture. A large portico circles halfway around the house. There are three stories of rooms and living space, as well as an observation tower that stands five stories above the ground. The house would eventually get gas lighting, running water, and central heat from a furnace long before any of these conveniences were commonplace.

When the Milford Historical Society purchased the house, they painstakingly restored it to how it was when Governor Pattison lived there from 1879 to 1906.

ghost story

Many strange things happen inside this house. The phenomenon that is reported most often is the sound of footsteps when no one is around to make them. These phantom footsteps are reported all over the building, especially on floors above where the witness is standing. Other times, people will report that items in the house have been moved around despite the building having been locked up for the evening. Also, there is a mysterious woman who haunts the building. Sometimes she is seen by witnesses inside, but most of the time she is seen from the outside, standing at the observation room at the top of the five-story tower.

visiting

On Friday, Saturday, and Sunday, Promont House is open to the public for tours. Admission is five dollars. It's open from 1:30 to 4:30 on these three days, and this is a wonderful opportunity for you to enter the house, looking and listening for the resident ghosts.

If you don't have a chance to make it to the building during these hours, there is still the chance that you can see that apparition of the woman if you visit the site at another time. Since she is often seen in the windows at the top of the observation tower, you could always just wait outside and look up at those windows in hopes of seeing her.

TAFT MUSEUM OF ART

316 Pike Street, Cincinnati, OH 45202

directions

Located in downtown Cincinnati, the Taft is a few blocks from the center of the city. Follow Fifth Street east (it's one way) until just past the Taft Theater. Turn right onto Pike Street. The Taft Museum of Art will be on your left. There is a parking garage behind the building.

history

This building was built as a house in 1820 by a man named Martin Baum, who would become an important figure in Cincinnati history because he is responsible for bringing many Germans to the city to work at his businesses, accounting for the large German population in Cincinnati today. Eventually, though, Baum went bankrupt and lost the house.

The house was then bought by a man named David Sinton, who eventually gave it to his daughter Anna and her new husband Charlie Taft (the brother of President William Howard Taft). The Tafts lived in the house for many years, all the while collecting art. In 1927, the Tafts gave the house to the city of Cincinnati to be used as an art museum in the heart of downtown. The house has operated continuously as a museum through the present day.

ghost story

Many strange things happen throughout the museum. People will see strange figures or hear footsteps echoing throughout the hallways. Probably one of the most frequently reported hauntings takes place in the gift shop. The person who opens the gift shop in the morning will find that many items have fallen from the shelves onto the floor. This happens so often that the person closing up the shop for the night will make sure that nothing is perched precariously on the edges of any shelves. Despite these extra precautions, the items still somehow fall from the shelves at night.

The most widely reported figure in the building is the "woman in pink." Some people claim she is the ghost of Anna Taft. She appears on the balcony in the back of the building, most often when there is some sort of event in the courtyard. People will recognize her from old photographs.

Other times, people will see Anna walking through the hallways of the house in a pink dress. She will seem as surprised to see the visitors as they are to see her. She will run into a room and slam the door behind her. When someone tries to check that room, a chair has been shoved underneath the door handle. When they are finally able to get the door open, they find the room empty. There are no exits to the room. Even the windows have long ago been painted shut.

visiting

The museum is closed on Mondays and Tuesdays, but it is open from eleven a.m. until five p.m. the rest of the week. Admission is eight dollars for adults and six dollars for students. It is free for anyone under eighteen years of age. The best way to investigate the building is to simply pay admission and enter during regular museum hours. Be aware that you are not allowed to take photographs within the building, so if you happen to see Anna, you won't be able to take her picture.

Make sure you visit the courtyard and look up to the haunted balcony and visit the haunted gift shop while you're there.

20TH CENTURY THEATER

3021 Madison Road, Cincinnati, OH 45209

directions

Take I-71 north to exit 6. Take exit 6 and take a right onto Edmondson Road. Then take a right onto Edwards Road (US-561). After following Edwards Road for about a quarter mile, take a sharp left onto Madison Road. Go approximately one mile until you reach the Oakley business district. The 20th Century Theater is on the right side. You can't miss the huge marquee.

history

The 20th Century was built in August of 1941, and it debuted with the film *Blood and Sand*. It continued to be a popular neighborhood theater in Oakley until 1983, when, like many single-screen neighborhood theaters, it closed down in the face of overwhelming competition from the larger multiplex theaters. For a while, the building sat abandoned. In 1990, a group in Oakley tried to have the building demolished, but a business owner purchased the structure and turned it into a flooring store. In 1992, it became the Oakley Church of Christ. Today it is used as a venue for concerts, weddings, and parties.

ghost story

The most famous ghost of the building is that of a projectionist who died in the projection booth. The stories say that when he missed a reel change, worried patrons went to the booth and found that he had died of a heart attack. Whether or not the story is true, strange things will often happen in the old projection booth. People will hear footsteps when there is no one near. People will see figures or smell strange scents while in the booth. People also will feel something touch them when no one is around.

The area now called the VIP room is allegedly haunted. It used to be a storage room that held projection equipment, but today it contains a bar and a pool table. People will see figures walk around and then disappear in the room. Locked doors will open by themselves.

One event that fueled the theory that the theater is haunted occurred when a man brought his dogs into the building. The dogs went crazy, jumping and barking until they escaped their owner and ran out the door. The owner gave chase, and he found the dogs sitting calmly outside the theater. They refused to come back inside.

visiting

An easy way to spend time in this wonderful theater is to rent it for a party—a ghosthunting party. If you're not ready to take on that commitment or expense, you could feign interest in renting the building and take a quick tour. The theater also hosts many events that are open to the public. It's entirely possible to experience paranormal activity at one of these events.

The owners of the theater are somewhat open to allowing established paranormal groups to investigate the building. If you are part of a paranormal group, you may want to ask the owners if they would allow you to investigate the site.

MUSIC HALL

1243 Elm Street, Cincinnati, OH 45202

directions

Take I-75 north to the Ezzard Charles Drive exit and turn right toward the city. Music Hall is the large reddish-brown structure at which Ezzard Charles Drive dead-ends on its eastern side.

history

The building was constructed in 1878, and from that year onward became a pinnacle of Cincinnati culture and society. Several Industrial Expositions (World's Fairs) were held at this building between 1878 until the largest and most elaborate of Cincinnati's expositions was held in 1888. The 1888 Industrial Exposition transformed the entire canal that ran adjacent to the building into the streets of Venice, complete with gondolas. A few years before, in 1884, one of the deadliest riots in the history of the country originated at Music Hall. A mob gathered at Music Hall to protest the lenient sentencing of a murderer. The mob felt that the murderer deserved to die instead of simply spending time in jail, so they decided to storm the courthouse down the street from Music Hall and kill him. They broke into the courthouse, killed all the condemned criminals who were being housed there, and burned the building to the ground. The National Guard was called to quell the rioters. Guardsmen killed many in the mob while trying to restore order. More than fifty people were killed in the rioting. The murderer who had started the incident was not among the dead; he had been moved to Dayton before the riot began. Perhaps the emotion involved when the mob met at Music Hall to decide their course of action has left some sort of imprint upon the property.

Many other events have occurred at the building over the years, making it the cultural center of Cincinnati. Today, Music Hall is the headquarters of the Cincinnati Symphony Orchestra, which regularly holds concerts in the building.

The darker history of Music Hall has more to do with what was at the location before the building was constructed. There was an orphanage at the north end of the site until the 1860s. It was dangerously under-funded, and there were several orphans who died as a result of poor supervision. They fell into the canal that ran next to the asylum and, being unable to swim, drowned there. Also, the first hospital in the city was either at the site of Music Hall or was directly across the canal. In the early days of the hospital, people were kept there essentially to quarantine them. In short, people were sent there to die.

Until Music Hall was built, there was a potter's field (or pauper's graveyard) at the south side of the site. In 1988, during restoration in the freight elevator shaft, workers found bones from this potter's field. Apparently, when the graveyard was moved to make way for Music Hall, several bodies were not discovered and were therefore not moved. There are likely more human remains underneath Music Hall to this day.

ghost story

The most famous ghost of Music Hall haunts the freight elevator. Although it requires a key to operate, the elevator sometimes will move up and down by itself. Other times, people will hear angry whispers and voices coming from within the elevator even though no one is in it.

There are many other ghostly stories attached to this building. Most of the stories concern footsteps or slamming doors. There is a team of security guards who work the building through the night. Many times when they are doing their rounds, they will hear a door slam that they were certain was locked and secured, or they will hear footsteps echoing down an empty corridor. The guards have heard a woman singing from an empty auditorium, they have found lights turned on that they know had been turned off.

visiting

This location is unfortunately quite difficult to visit with the intention of looking for the notorious spirits. On most days, the building is closed to the public, and management does not offer tours to the public. The only sure way to get in is to attend a public event—a concert or performance or charity function. Even when you've bought a ticket, you're not free to roam the building and explore.

If you are part of a ghosthunting group, it is possible to investigate the building, but it will cost you a lot of money. Last I heard, it costs about 800 or 900 dollars to do an investigation for a few hours at night. The cost is so high because a security staff must be there at all times when people are in the building. Most of your fee will pay for security. I have only heard of one group actually mounting an investigation at Music Hall, so I don't know if they will continue to allow groups to investigate there for the fee or not. If you are interested and can afford the price, contact the office at Music Hall

RAVE CINEMAS WESTERN HILLS

5870 Harrison Avenue, Cincinnati, OH 45248

directions

Take I-75 north to I-74 west to the Harrison Avenue/Rybolt Road exit. Turn left and take Harrison Avenue up the hill for a couple of miles. The theater will be on your left. The marquee is easily visible from the street.

history

There is really not much history to discuss about the building. Before the theater was built in 1994, the area was used as parkland, providing shelters for picnics. Before that, it was farmland and before that Native Americans roamed the area. The building is a fourteen-screen multiplex theater and a popular spot for west-side movie fans. At one point, the hillside behind the wing on the right side of the building began to fall away, and the building itself started to dip down with the hill, but the hillside was bolstered, and the structure was saved from catastrophic collapse.

ghost story

Several ghost stories are told about this theater. Most of those stories focus on theater ten, which is located on the hallway on the right side of the building and is the last door on your left. Sometimes the ceiling panels in this theater will come out by themselves. The ceiling is very tall, and management needs to build scaffolding to access the ceiling and replace the tiles. There is no way that a customer would be able to remove these tiles.

Managers claim that sometimes while they are watching a movie late at night when they are alone in the building they will turn around and see that they are not alone. A man will be sitting several rows back, watching the movie with them. The manager will be startled for a moment, and then the figure disappears.

I used to work as a manager in this building, and I have seen a ghost here. I was doing a maintenance shift with several ushers late one night, and I saw a figure walk across the lobby. An usher saw the same figure—a man in a dark jacket. We searched the building and found that the doors were locked and there was no sign of an intruder.

visiting

The building is open to the public, but to walk down to the haunted theater ten, you need to purchase a ticket for the show. Ticket prices are constantly changing, so all I can tell you is that it is cheaper to go to a movie during the day than at night, but it is creepier to sit alone in theater ten at night.

Your best chance of being alone in theater ten at night is to go during the week and hope that the film playing in theater ten is an unpopular movie. It happens frequently during the week that the theater is empty—or nearly empty—for the last show on a weekday.

SORG OPERA HOUSE
57 South Main Street, Middletown, OH 45044

directions
Take I-75 north to exit 19, the Union Center Boulevard exit. Turn left on Union Center Boulevard and follow the road for about three miles before turning right onto OH-747/Princeton Glendale Road. Follow this road for six miles before turning right onto Wright Brothers Memorial Highway/Hamilton Middletown Road/OH-4 North. Follow this road for another seven miles and then turn left on Second Avenue. Turn right onto Main Street. The Sorg Opera House will be on your right.

history
This building, built in 1891, is one of the oldest stage theaters in the country that is still in operation. The theater was built by Paul J. Sorg, an incredibly wealthy man who made his money in the tobacco industry. He built the theater for his wife, who loved opera. When it was built, it was one of the largest theaters in the country, featuring a floor section and two balconies. During the late 1800s and the early part of the twentieth century, African-American patrons who wanted to see the performances were forced to sit in the upper balcony of the theater.

From 1915 until the 1980s, the Sorg featured movies, but when the multiplex theaters took the market from single-screen theaters, the Sorg went back to offering stage productions. The upper balcony fell into disrepair and was eventually blocked off from the rest of the theater by a false ceiling.

ghost story
It is considered good luck for a theater to be haunted, and many theaters throughout the Cincinnati area are indeed reputed to host paranormal activity. The Sorg Opera

House is one of them. In fact, it may be one of the most famous haunted theaters in the entire state.

The most commonly reported phenomenon here is the sound of phantom footsteps. People will often hear footsteps echoing throughout the theater even when the place is empty. These witnesses will search the building but will find no source for the sounds. Other times people will feel like they are being watched or they will feel a hand touch them on the shoulder, only to turn around to find no one there.

At least four apparitions have also been sighted in the building. The most commonly reported apparition is that of Paul J. Sorg himself. He is often seen walking through the theater. Sometimes he is seen up on the catwalks above the stage. Other times he is seen in the theater area or in the dressing room area in the basement. People know that it is Paul Sorg because the apparition closely resembles his portrait that hangs in the lobby.

There is also a woman who is seen near the stage area. She is sometimes singing. People will hear singing coming from backstage even when the theater is supposedly empty. Other times she is sitting sadly in the area backstage. When she is seen, she is wearing either a red or a blue dress. She vanishes when she is approached.

The other two ghosts are not seen as often but do appear regularly. One is a bartender who is sometimes seen behind the bar. The other is an African-American man who is seen in the upper balcony area of the theater. He is seen sitting in a seat, looking down toward the stage, though that balcony has been closed off for years. Sometimes employees will leave a program in the upper balcony area for this ghost.

visiting

The theater opens only for events and keeps no regular hours. The owners, however, are interested in the ghosts and are open to inquiries regarding them. They sometimes hold haunted houses in the theater during the Halloween season, and they have allowed ghosthunting groups to conduct investigations of the paranormal activity here.

One way to enter the haunted theater is to simply attend one of the shows. If you want a more private look around, you may want to call the theater and ask if they are offering any tours or ghost hunts. On Halloween 2009, the theater offered an overnight stay at the haunted theater and they plan on offering this unique experience again on future Halloweens. If you are interested in this event, call to reserve your spot.

TAFT THEATER

317 East Fifth Street, Cincinnati, OH 45202

directions

The theater is located in downtown Cincinnati. Take Fifth Street to Main Street. The Taft Theater will be on your right just past Main Street. The marquee for the theater hangs over the sidewalk.

history

This theater was built in 1931 as a stage for plays. It features an art deco design, which was popular in that time period. Thousands of performances have been staged here over the years, including plays, musical and comedy shows. Today it is run by Live Nation, a group that books acts to perform at the venue. It is as popular today as it was when it first opened.

ghost story

All of the ghost stories at this theater focus on the balcony area, and many of them involve phantom smells. People will smell cigar smoke in the balcony, although no one has smoked a cigar in the theater for quite some time.

Other reports of ghostly activity in the theater involve a full-figure apparition which people will witness from time to time. People will see a man standing in the balcony area wearing a top hat. When they investigate, the man is never found. He simply vanishes into thin air. People assume that the man in the top hat is the reason for the phantom cigar smoke smell that often lingers in the balcony. Perhaps this man is an actor who has come back from the grave in full costume, or perhaps he was once an avid theater goer from the earlier years of the theater, come back to one of his favorite haunts.

visiting

To enter this location, you pretty much need to purchase a ticket for whatever event is playing at the theater. While writing this book and my previous book, I repeatedly have attempted to gain entrance just to see it and take some photographs, but Live Nation would not allow me to do that. I have decided that the best way to see the ghost here is to purchase tickets and then arrive as early as possible for the show. If you go up to the balcony before the audience shows up you may be able to catch of whiff of cigar smoke or perhaps ever catch a glimpse of the elusive man in the top hat.

WALTON CREEK THEATER

4101 Walton Creek Road, Cincinnati, OH 45227

directions

From downtown Cincinnati, take Columbia Parkway/US-50 east. After following this road for ten miles, you will go through the town of Mariemont. Just past Mariemont, where the road is no longer divided by a grassy median, turn left onto Walton Creek Road. You cannot miss the theater; it is the creepy-looking building directly in front of you at the first fork in the road. There is a sign out front advertising the Mariemont Players.

history

Several tribes of Native Americans lived on the land here. Mound-builders such as the Hopewells occupied the area for many years. More recently, the Shawnee hunted and fished in the area of the Walton Creek Theater and the adjacent river.

The original building here was a school, which was built in 1869. It was rebuilt in 1910 and continued to be a school for several decades. In 1958, a theater troupe known as the Mariemont Players purchased the building as a permanent theater for only $13,000.

Since 1958, the building has undergone numerous renovations and redesigns, but it still houses the Mariemont Players.

ghost story

The ghost here seems to be quite angry with those who enter the building. People will hear whispers from unknown sources telling them to get out. Recently, this phenomenon was reported by a sound technician who was working on a production. He left the building in terror as these phantom voices whispered to him.

Other people have reported feeling uncomfortable inside the theater, as if there is a presence that doesn't want them to be there. Most often, these whispers and feelings of discomfort are experienced in the basement of the building.

People also claim to see actual apparitions throughout the theater. Many of these apparitions will be those of Native Americans, although sometimes people will see small children dressed in nineteenth century clothing—perhaps ghosts of those children who once used this building as a school. These apparitions always vanish when they are approached.

visiting

You will need to purchase tickets to a show in order to gain access to the building. When there is a show playing at the theater, it is open Thursday through Sunday. On Thursday, Friday, and Saturday, the show opens at eight o'clock, and on Sunday it opens at seven. Tickets are seventeen dollars. Since everyone in the building is constantly busy setting up for the next show, they do not have time to take people through the building in off hours to look for ghosts, so your best chance of encountering one of these spirits is to actually purchase tickets and explore while you are waiting for your show to begin.

SECTION V

businesses

It seems that ghosts recently have become big business. With all the television shows, movies, and books about the paranormal these days, if you have a haunted business, you are able to make some money. But is having the uninvited spirit in your place of business really worth the money?

BIGG'S AT THE SKYTOP PAVILION

5218 Beechmont Avenue, Cincinnati, OH 45230

directions

From downtown Cincinnati, take Columbia Parkway to the east. Follow Columbia Parkway for about seven and a half miles and take the OH-32/Beechmont Avenue exit off the parkway. Stay straight off of the exit ramp. This road will eventually become Beechmont Avenue. The Bigg's will be about a mile and a half down the road on your left.

history

Everyone who remembers the hotel that used to be at the site of the Bigg's at the bottom of Beechmont Avenue seems to have his or her own memories and opinions about it. It was called the El Rancho Rankin, and depending upon whom you talked to from the early 1940s when it was built to the mid 1990s when it was destroyed, it was either an eyesore or a historic landmark in the small east-side town of Mt. Washington.

Mr. Rankin himself, the owner of the hotel, was somewhat eccentric. He built the hotel in the last days of the Great Depression, and through the years he decorated it with a menagerie of fiberglass animals. During most of its life the hotel was a decent place to stay the night or drink at the on-site bar. Eventually, though, the hotel's reputation faded, and it became a refuge for the area's poor and destitute. It developed a reputation as a seedy place to go. Several shootings took place on the property along with drug and prostitution arrests. The once iconic gaudy landmark had become a dangerous place.

Soon after Mr. Rankin died in 1995, the Mt. Washington fire department declared the building a firetrap and decreed that it be demolished. Many people were evicted from their homes and a piece of Cincinnati history was razed. Several years later, plans were finalized to build the Skytop Pavilion on the site where the El Rancho Rankin once stood. The centerpiece of this new development was the new Bigg's store.

ghost story

It's not often that you hear about haunted grocery stores. It is even rarer that they would be part of large chains like Bigg's, but strange things tend to happen at this store at the bottom of Beechmont Avenue in Mt. Washington.

The most commonly witnessed phenomena in this store are full-figure apparitions. These ghosts tend to be dressed in a way that witnesses describe as a little out of the ordinary, wearing suits and dresses that appear as if they were straight out of the 1950s. Something doesn't look quite right about these people. Many times these apparitions will turn the corner down one of the aisles and then the witness will turn the same corner and find that the apparition has vanished. Other times, the apparitions will vanish in front of people or will walk through a row of shelves or a wall.

Items will often fall from the shelves in the store, and employees will leave an aisle clean and then later return to the aisle only to find several items on the floor.

Many people who know the history of the site itself attribute these phenomena to ghosts from the El Rancho Rankin motel that stood here not too long ago.

visiting

Unfortunately, this Bigg's store is not open twenty-four hours a day. It is open until eleven p.m., however, so it is possible to try to see a ghost long after the sun has set for the night. Most of the time, the ghosts are seen after the sun sets, so your best chance of running into one of these spirits is to enter the store after dark but before the store closes at eleven. If you get hungry while you're there, you can even pick up a snack for yourself.

BOBBY MACKEY'S MUSIC WORLD

44 Licking Pike, Wilder, KY 41071

directions

Take I-75 south into Kentucky to exit 191, the Twelfth Street/Covington exit. Follow the road straight until you get to KY-1120 East/West Twelfth Street. Turn left onto West Twelfth Street. Follow this road for a little more than a mile and then turn right onto Brighton Street. Then turn right again onto West Twelfth Street/KY-9. Continue to follow KY-9. Bobby Mackey's will be on your right.

history

This building began its existence as a slaughterhouse—a fittingly bloody beginning for a reputedly cursed piece of property. The slaughterhouse was built in the 1850s and continued to operate until it was abandoned in the 1890s.

It is here that some of the facts may have become intermingled with legends. According to the stories, Satanists took over the building and began using the basement to perform ritual animal sacrifices. They would discard many of the dead animals in the well in the basement. The stories go on to say that these Satanists were connected to the area's most famous homicide: the murder of Pearl Bryan.

Scott Jackson and Alonzo Walling killed Pearl by decapitating her with dental instruments. They were wealthy young men from the area who were in medical school, and one of them had gotten Pearl pregnant. They saw no other option than to kill her. Rumors began circulating that Walling and Jackson were involved with the Satanists who practiced in the old slaughterhouse, and they had murdered her as an offering to Satan. Her head was never found. It has been suggested that it was dropped down the well in the basement.

While this story alone would be enough to make a building haunted, many more incidents occurred here that add to the dark history of the building. During Prohibition, it became a speakeasy, where several murders allegedly occurred. Later, mobsters took control of the bar and more murders were supposedly committed.

In fact, until the building was purchased by Bobby Mackey, some rather unsavory people ran the place, and murders would apparently happen here quite often.

ghost story

Any discussion of Cincinnati area ghosts would not be complete without mentioning Bobby Mackey's Music World. The building has been the subject of several cable ghost shows and has been the subject of more than one book. Many ghost stories are told about this place, but for this book, I only can cover the most popular ones.

One of the best involves the jukebox in the nightclub area. It often turns on by itself and will play the "Anniversary Waltz," and no cause has ever been found for why the jukebox plays on its own.

People often will report seeing apparitions, which sometimes are thought to be the ghosts of Walling and Jackson, who people recognize from old pictures of the men. Other times, people will report seeing the ghost of Pearl Bryan—who is easy to recognize because she's missing her head.

People also see the ghost of a woman named Johanna. This apparition is often accompanied by the smell of rose perfume, reportedly the same brand of perfume that Johanna wore while she was still alive.

Beyond these stories, people will report phenomena anywhere from uncomfortable chills down their spine, to being shoved down stairs, to being completely possessed by some dark demonic force. Stories are told of at least one exorcism in the building, that of a caretaker who used to live on the property who believed that he was possessed by some dark demon.

visiting

Bobby Mackey is well aware of the ghosts on his property and has used these ghosts to bolster his business. There is a sign as you walk in saying that he is not responsible for any injuries caused by the ghosts. Many sources claim that this is the most haunted nightclub in the country, possibly the world. The activity here seems to happen in both the basement area and the nightclub area.

To experience these ghosts, you simply have to come here during business hours. Or you can rent the building for a day and conduct an investigation if you want, though it's not cheap to do. The current fee is $600 for an overnight investigation of the building.

For those of you who want to see these ghosts but do not have that kind of a bankroll, the Northern Kentucky Paranormal Society and the Cincinnati Regional Association for Paranormal Studies conduct tours during the weekends for just ten dollars.

CROW'S NEST

4544 West Eighth Street, Cincinnati, OH 45238

directions

Take US-50/River Road west toward the Elberon/Warsaw exit. Exit US-50 onto Elberon Avenue and follow it for a little more than a mile until you get to the stop light at West Eighth Street. Turn left onto West Eighth Street and follow it for about two miles. The Crow's Nest will be on your right, just before Old Saint Joseph's Cemetery.

history

The Crow's Nest is named after the original owners of the bar who constructed the building in 1895. The owner's name was Mike Crowe, and he ran the bar with his wife. The bar survived Prohibition, the Great Depression, and all of the other hardships of the twentieth century and is still in operation today as the second-longest-running bar on the west side of Cincinnati.

ghost story

There is a general consensus that at least a couple of the ghosts in this building are those of the original owners, Mike Crowe and his wife. The couple still seems to be quite in love with one another and with the building itself, even after all these years. Although the third floor of the building is now an apartment and is completely off limits to the public, there are those who still see the happy couple on the third floor, either through the windows from the street or while in the apartment themselves. These witnesses will see the shadows of a couple dancing across the floor. The shadows will be cast across the walls and the floor and will be accentuated by the headlights of passing vehicles, but there are no figures seen who could be casting the mysterious shadows.

Paranormal activity also occurs in the areas of the bar still open to the public. Lights flicker on and off by themselves. Small items, such as keys and remote controls, disappear and then reappear in an unusual place elsewhere in the bar. A previous owner of the bar once was in one of the storage closets when the door suddenly slammed shut behind her, closing her in. She tried to open the door but was unable to for several minutes despite the fact that the door had no lock.

The basement also seems to be a hotbed of paranormal activity. Employees who venture into the basement are often assaulted by feelings of discomfort. A figure of a young man will sometimes be seen sitting on the stairs leading down to the basement, but he will vanish suddenly when approached or spoken to. The lights will flicker on and off in the basement, often for long periods of time.

visiting

This bar is open to the public from 11 a.m. to 2:30 a.m. every day of the week. It is still an active bar and restaurant, so you can enter during these hours, get yourself a drink, and experience the ghostly ambiance of the building.

Unfortunately, the third floor and the basement are closed to the public, so the ghosts that have been reported in these areas will be inaccessible. That's okay, though, since the rest of this historic building has its own share of ghostly phenomena.

FAIRFIELD BOWLING LANES

5181 Dixie Highway, Fairfield, OH 45014

directions

Take I-75 north to I-275 west. Take I-275 to the Route 4 exit (exit 41). Turn north onto Route 4. The road will change its name to Dixie Highway. About four miles from the interstate, the Fairfield Bowling Lanes will be on your left. The haunted location is actually behind the bowling alley, in an area where a small creek used to run.

history

According to legend, a serial killer stalked the Fairfield area during the early 1800s. He would linger in the wooded areas just outside the town and would kill people who had wandered too far from civilization. Once he killed a mother and her three-year-old son by the creek in the area now directly behind the bowling alley. The woman was wearing a white dress, and the boy was wearing brown pants and a white shirt. According to those who still see the small boy to this day, he was also wearing a hat.

ghost story

It is not the bowling alley itself that is haunted but rather the remnants of an old creek bed directly behind it. People usually will see two apparitions walking near the ditch behind the bowling alley. The apparitions always appear the same. There will be a woman walking beside a young child. The woman will be dressed in white, while the boy will be wearing brown pants with a white shirt and a hat. People claiming to know nothing about the ghost story at this location will describe these two figures by the creek wearing exactly these clothes. The woman is always wearing white and the boy is always wearing brown pants and a hat.

Other stories are also reported near this creek bed. People will hear a child crying or a woman screaming even when there is no one nearby. Shadowy figures will move throughout the trees between the apartments and the bowling alley, especially at night, and people will feel uncomfortable near the creek. They will feel as if they are being watched by some unseen presence.

visiting

Since this haunting is outside the bowling alley, the area where the ghosts are often seen does not close. It is not illegal to go down to the creek in the middle of the night, looking for the ghost of the mother with her son. Since the ghosts are most often seen after dark, your best chance of spotting these apparitions is probably late at night when there is little activity in the area.

This area, however, is directly behind an apartment complex. If the people who live in the apartments see people hanging out in the area in the middle of the night, they may ask you what you're doing or call the police. If you go, be respectful to those who are sleeping nearby.

THE GOLDEN LAMB

27 Broadway Street, Lebanon, OH 45036

directions

Take I-71 north and exit at Lebanon/Lebanon Raceway/OH-48 (exit 28). Follow OH-48 N for about four miles until you see an exit for OH-123. Take the OH-123 ramp toward OH-48/US-42 S/Lebanon. At the end of the ramp, turn left onto East Main Street/OH-123. About a mile down the road, turn right onto South Broadway Street. The Golden Lamb will be on your left. There is a parking lot behind the building.

history

The hotel was originally named the Golden Lamb because many people in the early nineteenth century were illiterate. Businesses often would put a recognizable picture on the sign outside of their front door and name the business after the picture. Since the Golden Lamb was halfway between Cincinnati and the National Road (today Route 40 near Dayton and Columbus), many people would stop here on their way from the east or the north to Cincinnati. As a result, many famous people of the day stayed at the Golden Lamb.

The Golden Lamb is the longest-running business in the state of Ohio. It began operating in 1803, and the current building was built in 1815. It was originally a two-story structure, but over the years, many additions were made. Big names from the time, such as Mark Twain and Charles Dickens, have stayed in the hotel. Twelve presidents of the United States have stayed at the hotel: J.Q. Adams, William Henry and Benjamin Harrison, Garfield, McKinley, Grant, Hayes, Harding, Taft, Van Buren, Reagan, and G.W. Bush.

A man named Charles Sherman, a justice at the Ohio Supreme Court, passed away at the hotel in 1829. Famous senator and presidential candidate Henry Clay lost his daughter Eliza when she got sick and died at the inn.

A girl named Sarah Stubbs moved to the hotel after her father died. At the time, Sarah's uncle was the manager of the hotel, so Sarah and her mother stayed there. Unfortunately, they were not able to stay in a single room. They were forced to move throughout the building to accommodate paying guests. According to legend, the constant moving frustrated Sarah to no end. Today, a room is dedicated to her. It has been restored to how it likely appeared whenever Sarah stayed there. Several pieces of furniture and toys that Sarah actually owned are displayed inside the room.

ghost story

Many ghosts supposedly haunt the Golden Lamb. How could you not have ghosts in a place with so much history that has seen so many famous people come through?

The ghost of Sarah Stubbs is seen most often and has become the most famous one at the inn. Since she was upset by having to move around so frequently, never being able to call a single room her home, she continues to haunt the hotel. Her supernatural activity is most often witnessed on the fourth floor, in or near the room that has been dedicated to her. Pictures often fall from the walls by themselves. Toys and furniture will move around the room although no one has moved them. Sometimes people will see a ghostly girl walking the halls of the hotel—especially on the fourth floor.

Doors throughout the hotel will open and slam shut by themselves, and Sarah is usually blamed for the noise. Since Sarah lived to be an adult, some people argue that the ghostly girl who roams the building is actually Eliza Clay, who died inside the hotel when she was young. People have also seen the apparition of Charles Sherman who died in the hotel. He is described as a gaunt and gray man who is often seen in the hallways of the building.

visiting

If you'd like to stay the night in a haunted hotel, you couldn't go wrong with the Golden Lamb. The rooms are decorated with antique furniture that gives them a nineteenth-century feel. The rooms cost between $107 and $133, and each one is named after a famous guest who once stayed in that room. If you want to look for ghosts, you may want to rent a room and spend that evening taking in the historic (and sometimes creepy) ambiance of the place.

If you don't want to spend the money, you still can look for ghosts. Sarah's room is in a public section of the hotel. You can walk up to the fourth floor and see it. If you visit at night, however, you need to be quiet. The doors do not go all the way to the floor, so any sounds are going to be heard by people staying in the hotel. Your best bet may be to go up in the early evening, after the sun has gone down but before everyone goes to sleep. You may want to ask permission from the front desk first as well. The employees I talked to at the hotel were very open and excited about their ghosts and were more than willing to let me go up to Sarah's room to see if she was there waiting for me.

HABITS CAFE

3036 Madison Road, Cincinnati, OH 45209

directions

Take I-71 north until you get to exit 6. Take exit 6 and take a right onto Edmondson Road. Then take a right onto Edwards Road (US-561). After following Edwards Road for about a quarter mile, take a left onto Madison Road. Habit's Café is on the left side of the road, across the street from the 20th Century Theater's huge marquee.

history

Some of the dark history of this location is vague and unclear since it deals with illegal operations that were kept off the books. Historic proof of some of the stories is impossible to verify. We do know that in the first half of the twentieth century, this building was known as Luke's Lounge, but beyond that, we only have local legends, which may or may not be true.

According to legend, the owner of Luke's Lounge was involved in a series of illegal fencing operations in the 1940s, and these operations were conducted out of the lounge itself. In order to guarantee himself some defense against the law, the owner paid off a crooked cop to help him with these illegal operations. One day, the police officer was shot dead in the basement of the building. The owner had mafia ties and a series of burglary convictions so he was immediately suspected of the crime. The police could never gather sufficient evidence to arrest him, however. In retribution, a family member of the owner was shot to death in the alley near the bar.

ghost story

Most of the ghost stories from this building focus on the basement where the police officer was supposedly shot. People will sometimes hear phantom footsteps echoing throughout the basement, though no one is down there. Other times people will see full apparitions moving around in the basement. The most famous of these spirits is that of a man wearing a white zoot suit and a fedora who vanishes when he is approached.

Many other strange occurrences happen in the basement of the building. All kinds of electrical equipment will malfunction when used within the basement. Also, strange glowing balls of light will hover around and then mysteriously disappear.

visiting

It is easy to visit Habit's Café but hard to access the haunted basement. The bar is popular and well worth the trip, but the basement is unfinished and therefore somewhat dangerous. The owner of Habit's understandably doesn't want to risk being held liable for anyone who gets hurt in the basement.

Several ghosthunting groups have been granted access to the basement, though these groups have signed liability waivers and other legal documents. If you are part of a ghost investigation group, it couldn't hurt to contact the owner and ask permission to access the basement. Otherwise, you may only be able to access the bar and restaurant area of the building.

HYDE PARK GRAETER'S ICE CREAM SHOP

2704 Erie Avenue, Cincinnati, OH 45208

directions

Take I-71 north until you get to exit 6 (Smith Road/Edwards Road/OH-561). Turn right off the exit onto Edmundson Road, and then turn right onto Edwards Road. Turn left onto Erie Avenue. When you turn, the road will be split by a wide median. Graeter's will be on your left near the corner. You can either park across the street from the store, or you can pull a U-turn after the median ends and park directly in front of the store.

history

Graeter's Ice Cream was founded near the beginning of the twentieth century. The owners utilized the French pot method for making ice cream, which made for a very thick and popular ice cream. The Hyde Park Graeter's opened in 1922, and it is now the oldest one in the world. It is still a popular destination for people of all ages throughout the city.

ghost story

Many people will see a ghost inside or near this ice cream shop. The ghost will be seen in many different places, doing many different things, but she will always look the same. She will appear as a young woman in a 1920s dress. Sometimes, people will see her inside the building while the shop is open for business. She will keep to herself in a remote corner. If she is approached, she vanishes.

Other times people will see her after the store has closed for the night. They either will be walking by on the street and happen to glance into the store to see a young woman in 1920s dress sitting inside, or they will see her walking around outside the building. Sometimes they actually see her walk through the front door. (And by through I don't mean opening up the door and walking in—I mean she literally walks through the front door at night sometimes.)

visiting

This ghost is easy to visit. Since she sometimes appears during business hours, you can always walk into the store, get yourself an ice cream, and wait for her to show up. It's also possible to spot this ghost long after the shop has closed. The large front windows expose most of the shop. Also, since the ghost sometimes is seen outside at night, you might see her on the street long after most of the residents of Hyde Park have fallen asleep.

LATITUDES
18 Main Street, Milford, OH 45150

directions
From downtown Cincinnati, take I-71 north to Kenwood Road, exit 11. Turn right onto Kenwood Road and follow that for almost a mile until you reach Shawnee Run Road. Turn left on Shawnee Run Road. Shawnee Run appears to dead end into Camargo Road, but if you turn right onto Camargo you can then make an immediate left onto the continuation of Shawnee Run. After following Shawnee Run for a little more than four miles, turn right onto Glendale/Milford Road or OH-126. Turn left onto Route 50. When you get to the second road on your left, you'll see Latitudes on the corner.

history
This bar had an important place in the history of the town of Milford. It was built as the town hall in 1891, though at that time the building appeared much different than it does today. It was a brown brick structure that stood three stories tall and featured a turret. It was originally used to house the city council of Milford, but over the years, many different government agencies have resided in this building.

By 1923, the top section of the building was ruled unsafe and the turret and third story were removed. By the late 1940s, Milford's fire and police departments were housed in the building. Eventually, the government agencies all moved away, and the location became the bar and restaurant that it is today.

ghost story

Perhaps the reason so many strange occurrences are recorded here is because of the building's importance to the history of Milford. The variety of these occurrences implies that several spirits haunt the place.

Many things throughout the building will move on their own. Bar stools will fall over and move across the bar for no reason. Doors will open and close by themselves and lock by themselves. There are reports of things such as ice scoops and glasses moving around on their own. Faucets will turn on by themselves, especially in the women's restroom in the downstairs area. People will hear footsteps even when the building is empty.

Full-body apparitions are also seen from time to time inside of the building. There isn't a particular one that is seen more often than another, but several have gained notoriety. A female figure was once seen standing by a table for a long period of time. A man was seen in an office but vanished shortly thereafter. There are ghosts in every corner and of almost every variety in this bar.

visiting

To access this building, you will need to arrive at the bar during normal business hours. Luckily, those hours run long into the night, so you can be here when the ghosts are most prevalent. On Sundays, the bar opens at noon and is open until two a.m., and the rest of the week it opens at 4:30 p.m. and remains open until two.

Many of the ghost stories occur in the main bar area. There are a couple of areas where ghostly activity takes place that are not open to the public, but there are so many things going on in this bar that you'll find plenty to see in the areas that are open.

McCLUNG HOUSE

105 East Main Street, Mason, OH 45040

directions

Take I-71 north to the Fields Ertel exit (exit 19). At the end of the exit ramp, turn left onto Mason-Montgomery Road. Follow Mason-Montgomery for about four and a half miles until you get to the intersection with Reading Road (US-42). The house is on the corner. At the time this book was written, there was both a café and a cake store inside the building.

From I-75, take the Tylersville Road exit (exit 22). Turn right (east) onto Tylersville Road. Follow Tylersville for a little more than two and a half miles, then turn left onto Reading Road. Less than a mile down Reading, take a right onto Main Street. The restaurant is on the corner.

history

In 1870, this building was simply a house built on Main Street in Mason. For the next thirty years it remained a typical home, and nothing dark seems to have happened here.

But in 1901, things changed. John and Rebecca McClung were living in the house at the time. John was known to be an incredibly possessive husband who would not allow Rebecca to be seen in public. On that dark day in 1901, people heard screams coming from the house. When they went inside to investigate, they found John covered in blood and Rebecca beaten to death in her own bedroom. She had been killed with a piece of wood from the fireplace.

Everyone knew that John had killed her, and he was brought to trial for the murder. Somehow he was acquitted of the crime. He never went to prison for the murder that everyone was sure he had committed. Rebecca was buried just down the street at Rose

Hill Cemetery (see the Rose Hill Cemetery chapter in the Cemeteries section of this book). John was later buried in the same plot.

Other families owned the house over the years. At one point it was a hotel until August of 2002 when it became the Chokolate Morel restaurant, which quickly gained a reputation for being haunted. No matter what the owners of the building tried, they couldn't remove the bloodstains from the floor where Rebecca was killed. Today the building houses both a café and a cake shop. Rumor has it that the bloodstains are still there.

ghost story

There are many reports of Rebecca haunting this house. According to legend, when John kept Rebecca locked away from everyone else, she would stand in the window of the upstairs bedroom, looking down at the world she was missing. Even today, more than a hundred years after she was killed, people will see her standing in that window gazing at the street below. Other times, her spirit will be felt, or she will be seen inside the room where she was murdered. People will also sometimes see her push items to the floor, and still others have reported that a figure of a woman approaches them menacingly and then suddenly disappears.

When she was killed, her body was moved to the basement so that her burial plot could be prepared. The ghost of Rebecca also haunts the basement. People will feel uncomfortable there, as if they are not welcome or are being watched. Sometimes employees will claim that they heard a female voice whispering their name, even when the basement is empty.

visiting

From a ghosthunter's point of view, there are positive and negative points regarding access to this building. On the positive side, the ghost has been seen many times from the outside as she stands at the upstairs window, so you can go there at any hour of the night and try to see her. Also many of the people who work there are familiar with the ghost stories about the building. If you visit as a customer and ask about Rebecca, the staff will be happy to tell you stories and may even show you around inside.

On the negative side, much of the building is not open to the public. The two shops only occupy the front rooms on the first floor. Much of the building is inaccessible to the public, especially to amateur ghosthunters hoping to explore it. The best way to see Rebecca may just be to look into the windows from outside or to step inside for a coffee.

OMNI NETHERLAND PLAZA

35 West Fifth Street, Cincinnati, OH 45202

directions

This building is in downtown Cincinnati on Fifth Street. It is connected to the Carew Tower.

history

This building was constructed in 1931 with a beautiful art deco design alongside the Carew Tower, which stands next to it. It is a popular luxury hotel where many famous people have stayed. John F. Kennedy stayed here and attended an event in the Hall of Mirrors, the hotel's famous banquet hall. Franklin and Eleanor Roosevelt also stayed in the hotel, as did Elvis Presley and George H. W. Bush.

In 1961, the hotel was modernized. The original art deco décor was replaced with linoleum and wallpaper. By 1983, the owners realized that the hotel's charm was in its original décor, however, so they shut down for three years to restore the earlier design and decorations.

Some dark events have happened throughout the hotel's history. A woman named Jean Haller killed herself by jumping out of the twenty-eighth floor. A businessman died of a heart attack in the lobby. And perhaps the strangest reputed event to take place at the hotel was that during construction, a man fell from the building and mysteriously vanished. His wife would come to the site every day in a green dress looking for her husband.

ghost story

The most famous ghost at the hotel is the Lady in Green. Legend says that she is the wife of the man who fell from the building in 1931 during construction whose body was never found. His wife, in a green dress, supposedly still roams the halls looking for her lost husband. The first sightings of this apparition were in 1983 during its restoration. Workers would be going about their business and would sometimes see a woman in a vintage green dress watching them. Sometimes they would question her, and she would always disappear. The Lady in Green now is seen most often in the Hall of Mirrors on the mezzanine of the building.

The stairwell of the twenty-eighth floor also is reputedly haunted, most likely by the ghost of Jean Haller. People will hear sobbing coming from that stairwell and will also sometimes see the figure of a woman that mysteriously vanishes.

People also will hear phantom footsteps in the lobby, and sometimes some of the rooms will mess themselves up after housekeeping cleans them.

visiting

It's hard to say how to visit this location. Of course, you can rent a room for the night and hope that some ghostly activity occurs during your stay. This approach is kind of a crapshoot, however, because there is not a particular room or floor that is said to be haunted. The rooms that mess themselves up seem to be randomly scattered throughout the building.

It's possible to check out the stairwell on the twenty-eighth floor. Of course, this would be easiest if you already had a room, but even if you didn't, you could walk into the building and go to the stairwell. This approach would work better during the day because you would more easily blend in with the rest of the guests. At night, if the staff knew you didn't have a room, they may not want you there simply to look for a ghost.

The Hall of Mirrors is the hardest place to tell you how to visit. When I approached the lobby staff asking to photograph and enter the Hall of Mirrors as an author, they were more than happy to let me walk up and check out the room. Later, though, I called asking if they had any historic photos that I could use in my book, and they were very belligerent and hesitant to oblige. They claimed that they didn't want to promote their ghosts stories despite the fact that the Lady in Green is mentioned in their brochure. I would guess that it couldn't hurt to ask if you could check out the Hall of Mirrors. If they say no, the Lady in Green has been seen elsewhere, and you could always find your way up to the twenty-eighth floor.

PETER'S CARTRIDGE COMPANY

1915 Grandin Road, Kings Mills, OH 45039

directions

Take I-71 north to the Kings Mills exit (exit 25). Stay right on the exit until you get to Kings Mills Road, where you turn right. About half a mile down the road, turn right onto King Avenue. As you cross the Little Miami River, King Avenue changes its name to Grandin Road. Peter's Cartridge Company is the huge factory building just past the river. A bike trail runs between the factory and the Little Miami River.

history

For many years, Peter's Cartridge Company was the main reason why anyone lived in the small town known as Kings Mills. In the 1860s, this building was built as a munitions factory that helped supply the Union Army during the Civil War. It continued to be a munitions factory for many years. Eventually it went out of business and was purchased by Remington to make ammunition.

During the many years of the factory's operation, much of the town of Kings Mills was employed there, but by the time the factory went out of business, there were many other businesses in town, which continued to thrive. Today, Kings Mills is one of the premiere tourist spots in the Cincinnati area, with such popular attractions as Kings Island Amusement Park, Great Wolf Lodge, and the Beach Waterpark.

Despite its importance to the community, the factory has seen its share of tragedy. Many workers died in explosions at the site. Working with munitions is dangerous, of course, and in the 1800s there were far fewer safety regulations to protect the workers. The 1800s weren't the only years in which this factory experienced disaster, however. As recently as August of 1940, three men were killed in an explosion at the plant.

Today, the building houses several small businesses and at least one tenant who lives in an apartment within the building. Much of the building is falling into disrepair, and there are rumors of a Satanist cult that sometimes worships within the building.

ghost story

Many ghosts, supposedly of those who died in tragic accidents at this site, haunt the old munitions factory. People will hear footsteps on the upper floors of the building when the building is supposedly empty. Other times, people will hear footsteps above them on the roof of the building but will find no one there.

Today, the elevator shafts are hollow and decrepit. Old cables hang empty within these shafts. Many stories involve these cables moving by themselves without any reason.

Other ghosts are seen from the outside of the building. People on the adjacent bike trail will see figures standing in the upstairs windows that suddenly disappear. Other times, passersby will hear screams or industrial sounds coming from within the factory.

visiting

Do not enter this building! It is extremely well guarded and monitored by the owners as well as by the local police. Whatever excuse you use when you are caught, you will be prosecuted for trespassing. The only way to gain access is to get permission from the owners. They have granted access to people interested in the building's ghosts, but I wouldn't count on it. I would focus my energy on admiring the utter creepiness of the building as a whole and trying to experience the ghosts you can see from the outside. Spend time on the bike trail that runs along the building. People riding bikes along this trail have often reported activity within the factory, especially near dusk or later in the day. Stand on this trail and watch for figures in the windows and listen for sounds that don't belong.

REILY PIZZA

Corner of Main Street and Reily Millville Road,
Reily Township, OH 45056

directions

Take I-75 north to I-275 west. Take I-275 to the Colerain Avenue/US-27 exit and take US-27 north. Follow this road for about ten and a half miles past Ross until you are almost to the traffic light in Millville. Turn left onto OH-129/High Street. Follow OH-129 for about six miles and then turn right onto Sample Road/OH-732. Follow this road for about three miles. You'll enter the town of Reily. Sample Road dead-ends into Main Street. Turn right onto Main Street. Reily Pizza is one block down on the corner of Main Street and Reily Millville Road.

history

There is not much history to tell about the pizza parlor/bar that sits on the corner of Reily's Main Street. The building was built as a restaurant and has continued to be one. Any darker history that may have spawned the ghosts that supposedly haunt the building is confined to the history of the town.

Long ago, Reily was the site of an ancient Indian burial ground. This may seem like a ghost cliché, but it has been proven that the land in and around Reily was used by the ancient mound-building Native American cultures as a place to bury their dead. Two Native American burial mounds have been confirmed in Reily and the area just outside of town. One of these mounds is actually within the Reily Cemetery.

According to rumor, when Reily was settled by westerners, many of the original planners of the city were Satanists. Rumors go on to state that the first five businesses in Reily were built so that if one were to draw a line connecting them, they would take the shape of a satanic pentagram. These strange stories go on to suggest that Reily Pizza sits in the exact center of this pentagram (see the Reily Cemeteries chapter in the Cemeteries section of this book).

ghost story

Many people feel uncomfortable when inside or in the area immediately surrounding Reily Pizza. They say that even when they are just driving through in their cars they feel they are being watched by some evil presence. People will get chills down their spines and will constantly see movement near the building out of the corner of their eyes. When they turn their head to see the source of the movement, they see nothing.

Inside the building itself, an array of strange things supposedly occurs. The lights will flash on and off by themselves even long after the building has closed and emptied for the night. Glasses will move by themselves and will fall off of tables and the bar even when no one touches them. People will also hear commotion going on inside of the bar, which sounds like people talking, long after everyone has left the building.

visiting

Reily Pizza is kind of a hole-in-the-wall bar that likes to serve its regulars. Reily Pizza isn't the classiest restaurant in Southwest Ohio, but the people here are friendly. The staff, however, doesn't talk much about the ghosts that reside there. Visiting the exterior of this site long after the restaurant closes for the night may be a better way to experience the building's creepy nature. It is still possible to witness the shadowy figures that move around the site and the lights and sounds that supposedly go on inside the building, and there aren't other people around to mess with the mood.

Still, if you go there after closing time, don't go too close to the building. I wouldn't be comfortable walking up to the windows of the closed restaurant and looking in. Someone might misunderstand your intentions and call the police, who probably won't be happy with the 'looking for ghosts' excuse.

SHIMMERS BALLROOM AND TAVERN

1939 Dixie Highway, Ft. Wright, KY 41011

directions

Take I-75 south to exit 189 toward Ft. Wright/Park Hills. Turn right onto Kyles Lane. Then make a sharp left onto Dixie Highway/US-127. A half-mile down the road, you'll see the Shimmers Ballroom and Tavern on your left. When you park, pay close attention to what is hotel parking and what is Shimmers parking. The hotel apparently will tow the cars of Shimmers' patrons.

history

It seems that for a period in the tavern's history, crime was a problem. The ballroom started its dark history as a speakeasy during Prohibition. The proprietors illegally sold alcohol, and this practice attracted a criminal element.

At some point, the mafia supposedly became involved in the operation of the bar. During one dispute in the basement of the bar, a man was executed. The bar was also used as a brothel at one point during its history. In perhaps its most famous case,

Cincinnati mayor Jerry Springer was caught with a prostitute at the motel across the parking lot from Shimmers.

Today, Shimmers is quite different from its seedy origins. The building is now a ballroom and bar that is quite safe to enter.

ghost story

Several ghost stories are reported at the Shimmers Ballroom. Much of the activity here occurs in the basement, where the execution took place. People will often see shadow figures that will suddenly vanish. In other parts of the building, objects will move by themselves. Glasses will move in the bar area. Chairs and tables will move despite the fact that there is no one near them.

visiting

From what I understand, Shimmers embraces their history and is open to the possibility that there are ghosts on the property. At least one ghosthunting group has been allowed to investigate the basement of the building at night. If you are a part of a group and are interested in learning more about this location, ask the management if you can investigate the property.

If you just want to visit the site in an attempt to see the ghosts, the bar at Shimmers is open to the public throughout the week. On weekdays and Saturday, it is open until two a.m. On Sunday, it is open until midnight.

Unfortunately, the basement isn't normally open to the public. If you ask the right people during times when it's not busy, though, they would probably allow you to go down and have a look.

SMOKIN' MONKEY

3721 Harrison Avenue, Cincinnati, OH 45211

directions

Take I-74 west from Cincinnati to the Montana Avenue exit. Turn left onto Montana at the end of the exit ramp and follow Montana up the hill to Harrison Avenue. Turn right onto Harrison Avenue. The Smokin' Monkey will be on the left just past the Wendy's on Glenmore Avenue. The building looks abandoned from the outside, but the door to the bar is on the side of the building adjacent to the public parking lot.

history

The founder of Cheviot himself once owned the property where the Smokin' Monkey stands today. He lost his wife in a drowning accident and lost two sons to lightning strikes. They were buried in the area that is now the parking lot for the bar.

The bar itself also has a rather dark history. The building was likely used as a brothel and a gambling place during the more nefarious years of Cheviot's history. It is not impossible that dark deals went on within the building and that people were killed here.

ghost story

Strange things occur within the Smokin' Monkey. Most of the paranormal activity involves things moving around the bar during the night. Often the staff will leave an item in a certain place and then come back later to find that it has been moved. This will happen most often with an ice scoop that is left in a bin outside of the ice machine. The scoop will either end up on the floor or end up within the ice machine itself despite no one having touched it. The liquor bottles lined up behind the bar will sometimes turn by themselves. When the opening bartender comes in the next day, the labels on the bottles face away from the bar. Perhaps this ghostly activity is simply the ghosts partying here after the living element has left for the night.

Be that as it may, the most paranormally active place in the building is the basement. People have seen figures, heard footsteps, and witnessed lights flickering on and off for no reason, but most often what people don't like about the basement is the feeling they get when they enter. They feel they are being watched. They also feel chills creep down their spine and a general unwelcome feeling.

visiting

The bar area of the Smokin' Monkey is open evenings on Wednesday, Friday, and Saturday. Despite the lack of windows to the outside world, it is a nice place to go to grab a beer in a haunted bar. In October the Smokin' Monkey offers ghost tours of the property. Taking the tour is your best chance to get into the haunted basement.

SOUTHGATE HOUSE

24 East Third Street, Newport, KY 41071

directions

From downtown Cincinnati, take I-471 south into Kentucky to the first exit, exit 5 (KY-8/Newport). Follow the exit to the first light and then turn left onto Dave Cowens Drive/KY-8. At the next light, near the Newport on the Levee center, turn left onto Washington Avenue. Then at the next light turn right onto Third Street. The Southgate House will be on the left across from Newport on the Levee. Parking is available on nearby streets or there are several lots available at Newport on the Levee.

history

A man named Richard Southgate built the house in 1814. Through the years, the house has been a major fixture in the Newport area, and several events of some historical significance have occurred here. The inventor of the Tommy Gun, John Thompson, was born in the house in 1860. During the Civil War, General William Sherman stopped briefly at the house and threw a party with many of his officers on his way to fight the war in the South. The house was a social center and symbol of prestige in the area. Many important people have passed through these doors.

Today, the building is used as a music venue and a bar. The basement houses a large stage where bands often play. The first floor houses the main bar and a lounge where customers can sit. There is another lounge on the second floor and an art gallery on the third floor.

ghost story

The ghosts here at the Southgate House tend to be quite active. A week rarely goes by when something doesn't move by itself. Decorations will move across the floor. Glasses in the bar will rattle together even when there is no one nearby. People will hear footsteps and voices coming from the building even when it is empty. The front door will often open and close by itself. Many people attribute these ghostly occurrences to one of the three ghosts that have been seen throughout the building.

The first and most active ghost has been given the name Elizabeth. A legend is often told about the origins of Elizabeth, but it is unclear whether or not the story is true. Elizabeth was married to a man who worked on the riverboats on the nearby Ohio River. She would often climb to the widow's peak of the building and watch her husband's riverboat as it left and arrived. One day she watched in horror as her husband's riverboat exploded. The explosion was so intense that she knew no one could have survived. Crushed, she hung herself there in the widow's peak. Unfortunately, her suicide was completely needless. Her husband had been running late that day and had missed the riverboat. He wasn't on board when it exploded.

Many of the things that happen throughout the house are attributed to Elizabeth. When the front door opens and closes by itself, people say that's Elizabeth leaving for a walk. A piano in the upstairs of the house will sometimes begin playing music by itself, another phenomenon attributed to the ghost of Elizabeth.

Another ghost often seen at the Southgate House is a Civil War soldier wearing a Confederate uniform. He appears throughout the house and sometimes carries on conversations with people who assume he is a real man wearing a costume.

The third ghost is that of a small boy. People will see him running and playing throughout the house. When they try to chase him down, they are never able to find him. He mysteriously vanishes.

visiting

This building is easy to visit. Even when there are no concerts going on, the building operates as a bar. You can go in for a drink and then explore for the ghosts. Many of the sightings here have been made by patrons. Since it is easy to explore the building while it is open to the public, the simple act of entering may be the best way to find the ghosts.

U.S. PLAYING CARD COMPANY

4590 Beech Street, Cincinnati, Ohio 45212

directions

From downtown Cincinnati, take I-71 north to exit 6, the Smith Road/Edwards Road exit. At the end of the ramp, turn left onto Edmondson Road. A short distance down the road, turn right onto Melrose Avenue. After another quarter mile, turn left onto Beech Street. The building will be on your right. You cannot miss the large clock tower at the center.

history

While the U.S. Playing Card Company began operations in the late 1860s, the building that currently stands in Norwood was constructed in the early 1900s. The company was and still is the largest playing card manufacturer in the world, and before the headquarters of the company moved to Erlanger, Kentucky, years of constant activity and production has somehow left a spectral imprint upon the building itself.

Through the years that the Norwood factory was in operation, many accidents occurred, some of them fatal. As recently as 2002 a large, extremely heavy roll of paper somehow fell and rolled toward a female employee, pushing her into an elevator. The elevator could not support the weight of the paper and plummeted to the ground, killing the woman.

Today the factory is closed to production, but the building does house a museum of the history of the U.S. Playing Card Company and there are still several parts of the building that do operate to a limited extent.

ghost story

Most of the ghosts in this building are confined to an elevator far in the interior of the building. There were at least three fatalities in this elevator shaft, including the woman who died here in 2002, and many people say that she is the spirit who haunts this building.

People will feel uncomfortable when they are alone and near the elevator shaft. Other times people have taken photographs of the elevator shaft and have photographed strange glowing balls of light, even at times when there is no reason for any dust to have kicked up in the area.

Other times employees have seen figures walking near the elevator shaft that suddenly disappear. Sometimes workers see the figure of the woman who was killed out of the corner of their eyes near the elevator shaft but when they turn their heads to look, no one is there.

visiting

Unfortunately, the haunted section of this building is incredibly difficult for an amateur ghosthunter to access. That section is closed to the public. It is closely guarded. Since most operations have moved to a new factory in Erlanger, Kentucky, the public only has access to a front section where the small playing-card museum is located. While apparitions have been seen all over the building, the ghosts are most often spotted near the elevator shaft. It is always possible to ask someone for a tour of the building, but in my experience, it is not likely to succeed. This may be a ghost that is best left alone nowadays. If you want to enter the building, the museum is open Tuesday and Thursday from noon till four. Admission is free.

VERNON MANOR HOTEL

400 Oak Street, Cincinnati, OH 45219

directions

Take I-75 north to exit three, Hopple Street. This exit will be on the left side of the highway. Once you exit, take a left onto Hopple Street. Stay straight on the road, keeping to the left of the White Castle as you go up the hill. At this point, Hopple changes its name to Martin Luther King Drive. After following this road for a little more than two miles, turn right onto Reading Road. About a quarter mile down Reading, turn right onto Oak Street. The hotel is one block down the road on your right.

history

The hotel was built in 1924 and has been a favorite stop for wealthy people from Cincinnati and for visitors to the city. Two presidents, Lyndon Johnson and John Kennedy, stayed here, as did the Beatles, who had rooms on the sixth floor. The building, particularly its address, was featured prominently in the movie *Rain Man*, as the character played by Dustin Hoffman says over and over that he needs to buy underwear at a K-Mart located at 400 Oak Street—an inside joke with the staff of the hotel, where the cast and crew stayed during filming in Cincinnati. There are several rumors that the Vernon Manor was one of the inspirations for Stephen Kings novella *1408*.

A young woman who was left at the altar in the 1940s seems to be the origin of many of the ghost stories that come from this building. Crushed that her fiancé had left her and her life had been ruined, she opened the window near the elevator on the sixth floor and jumped to her death.

ghost story

Ghosts have been experienced all over this hotel. Strange voices and footsteps will be heard despite the fact that no one is there. People will see strange figures who walk up and down the hallways and then disappear. In the bar area, glasses will fall off the bar by themselves when there is no one nearby.

While the entire building is reputed to be haunted, most of the activity occurs on the sixth floor. In many of the rooms on this floor, people will feel uncomfortable throughout the night. Sometimes, people will wake up in the middle of the night and see figures standing in their rooms dressed in early twentieth century clothing. Other times people will feel someone sit on the bed with them but look up and see no one there. The water in the bathrooms on this floor will turn on by itself. The apparition seen most often on the sixth floor is that of a young woman wearing a white nightgown. Many people suggest that this figure and many of the other hauntings can be attributed to the young woman who killed herself by jumping out the sixth-floor window.

visiting

Sadly, the Vernon Manor Hotel went out of business in March of 2009. The building has been shut down and all access to the interior has been restricted. Large abandoned buildings in areas of such valuable real estate are in grave danger of being torn down, of course, but the building has become a Cincinnati landmark and is not likely to fall victim to demolition. Mayor Mark Mallory stayed in the hotel on its final night of operation and said that he will fight hard to protect the building. A number of uses have been discussed for the old hotel, including reopening it as a hotel. Maybe it will open again and those interested in staying in a haunted room will be able to reserve one on the sixth floor.

Until that time, however, this building is mostly off limits to ghosthunters. I haven't asked about it myself, but it is possible that a ghosthunting group with a nice bankroll may be able to call the building's owners and secure access, but otherwise there is no way to gain access to these ghosts. They'll have to talk among themselves until the building reopens.

WESTERN HILLS COUNTRY CLUB

5780 Cleves-Warsaw Pike, Cincinnati, OH 45233

directions

Take I-75 north to exit 2B, Harrison Avenue, on the left side of the highway. Take the Western Hills Viaduct and follow the signs that lead to Queen City Avenue. Follow Queen City Avenue to the left past the BP and go up the hill about a mile and a half until you get to the traffic light at Sunset Avenue. Turn left onto Sunset Avenue. After about a half mile, turn right onto Guerley Road. At the top of the hill, Guerley changes its name to Cleves-Warsaw. Continue to follow this road straight for another two miles. The country club and golf course will be on your right.

history

This country club was founded in 1912 and has since become a landmark in Western Hills. It is one of the oldest private clubs in Cincinnati and includes dining rooms, a bar, and a golf course. The neighborhood around the country club, especially on Neeb Road, includes some of the largest and most beautiful houses in the city. Most were built during the 1920s, and their original owners belonged to the Western Hills Country Club.

ghost story

There are a variety of small hauntings that occur in this building. Sometimes glasses in the bar area will fall from where they are being stored all by themselves. People will see ghostly figures in early twentieth century dress walking throughout the building. When approached, the figures fade away.

Sometimes at night, when all the customers have left, people will see a man dressed as an employee setting the tables in the dining room. When approached, he vanishes. If he is not approached, he finishes setting the tables and then disappears into the back of the building. Talk about a dedicated employee! Forget about calling in sick, these employees show up to work when they're dead!

visiting

It is very difficult to visit the site of this haunting. You need to work at the club, be a member of the club, or know a member of the club. Even if you meet one of these criteria, you would still be seriously hampered in your search for ghosts. You aren't allowed to just freely roam the building, and you wouldn't be allowed to go through the building with any type of equipment looking for ghosts. It is probably better to just drive by this location knowing that it's haunted and be satisfied with that.

WESTERN WOODS MALL (DILLARD'S)

6290 Glenway Avenue, Cincinnati, OH 45211

directions

Take I-75 north to the Harrison Avenue exit (on the left) and follow the signs to Queen City Avenue. Follow Queen City to Sunset Avenue and turn left on Sunset. About a half-mile up Sunset turn right onto Guerley Road. At the first light you come to, turn right. That is Glenway Avenue, and Dillard's will be on your right a few miles down the road. If you get to the Friday's, you've gone too far.

history

There was once a mall here at the site of the Dillard's store. In fact, Dillard's was a store within this mall. There was also a pet store, a music store, and a number of other stores. Eventually, the mall shut down and the security guards who watched the property in the time immediately after the mall's closing in 1998 and 1999 began to report encounters with a ghost they called Charlie. The mall now is the Dillard's, a Home Depot, and a Spa Lady Fitness Center.

ghost story

Most of the ghost stories here involve people feeling a presence. A security guard once stated that he felt a presence in the fitting room area of the closed mall. Suddenly, the temperature dropped dramatically. He reported this to his supervisor, who investigated the fitting rooms skeptically—until she felt the exact same sensation.

According to legend, the security guards then somehow attempted to communicate with the spirit that they were sure haunted the building. The story says that they were able to successfully communicate with the spirit and determine that his name was Charlie.

Charlie has been seen and felt several times since then. Employees at Dillard's will see a man walking through the store after they have closed for the night. When they approach him, he vanishes. Most of these sightings occur near the back of the store, closer to where the main body of the Western Woods Mall once stood. I haven't run across any theories as to who this ghost could be.

visiting

Charlie isn't the easiest ghost to visit. Most of the sightings and experiences occurred in the old mall area of the building that is closed off to the public. Many more sightings have occurred inside the Dillard's but usually after the building has closed for the night.

In my opinion, you have two options of successfully encountering this ghost. The first option is to go into Dillard's while it is still open but after the sun has gone down and then browse the back of the store looking for strange male figures. The other option is to go to the mall late at night and park around the side of the building. At the side of the building is the old entrance to the mall. The doors are made of glass so you can still see into the old mall even though this area is closed off to the public. Perhaps here you can catch a glimpse of Charlie.

THE WHITE HOUSE INN

4940 Mulhauser Road, Hamilton, OH 45011

directions

Follow I-75 north from Cincinnati to I-275 west. Take I-275 to the SR-747 exit to the north, exit 42B. Follow 747 for a little more than a mile and a half and then turn right onto Mulhauser Road. Less than a half-mile down the road on your left, you will see a sign for the White House Inn restaurant.

history

While the White House Inn was not an overly important landmark in the area, it is an older building that was once a farmhouse in the southeastern corner of Butler County. More recently it was redesigned and converted into a restaurant. Seven of the rooms were restored to their original look and décor and today serve as dining rooms. Many ghost researchers believe that a significant amount of restoration work on an older building can kick up a lot of otherwise dormant ghostly activity. Perhaps this restoration is the reason that the ghost here has been seen so often since the restaurant opened.

ghost story

This building is haunted by the ghost of a little girl who is both seen and heard by employees and patrons. She appears throughout the house and has been seen on the grounds outside, especially near the gazebo. When people see her, she will turn a corner and disappear. If she is followed, there is never any sign of her. She is gone without a trace.

The girl is also heard from time to time. People will hear a child's laughter or will hear a small girl's voice, but when they investigate, they find no sign of her anywhere. Other times, things will move by themselves throughout the building. Glasses will clink together, silverware will become displaced at some point during the night, and other items throughout the house will move around the building.

visiting

Your best chance of gaining entrance to this building and encountering this ghost is to eat at the restaurant. The meals are a bit expensive for those on a tight budget, but the food is good and an entree rarely will cost more than twenty dollars. The building is open eleven till nine Tuesday through Thursday and is open until ten on Friday and Saturday. On Sunday, the building is open until seven, and it is closed on Mondays.

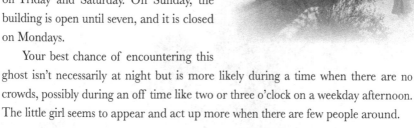

Your best chance of encountering this ghost isn't necessarily at night but is more likely during a time when there are no crowds, possibly during an off time like two or three o'clock on a weekday afternoon. The little girl seems to appear and act up more when there are few people around.

SECTION VI

schools and
public buildings

School and work: when you are
young the majority of your life seems
to be spent within a school building, and as
you get older, school is replaced by
your job. It seems only logical that once
we pass on, some of us will continue to
inhabit these places where most of our
waking hours were spent. Unfortunately,
there are very few of us who actually
enjoyed these places in life.

ANDERSON HIGH SCHOOL

7560 Forest Road, Cincinnati, OH 45255

directions

Take I-471 south to I-275 east. Take I-275 until you get to the Five Mile Road exit (exit 69). Turn west onto Five Mile Road and follow the road until you get to Beechmont Avenue. Turn right onto Beechmont Avenue. Stay on this road for less than a quarter mile, and turn right onto Forest Road. Anderson High School will be on your left.

history

The original building was built in 1964, but over the years additions have been made. These extensions enlarged the building and, when viewed from above, gave it the shape of a letter "A." There seems to be no dark history here at Anderson High School. No records exist of anyone who has died within these walls.

ghost story

The most famous ghost story of Anderson High School takes place at night once everyone has left the building. Some students will clearly remember leaving some of their belongings in a particular place. When they come in the next morning, they find that their belongings are gone. It is not until later that they discover that their belongings have been moved to another part of the building. Things will be moved from classroom to classroom or from locker to locker without any apparent reason.

Also, janitors at night will often hear children's voices echoing throughout the halls of the school. The voices are so clear and believable that the janitors will search the entire building, thinking that there are trespassers inside. They always find that the building is completely empty.

visiting

As in most schools, it is difficult to experience these ghosts for yourself. One way, of course, is to be a student at the school, but even if you are a student, the only way to really experience a ghost is to have your belongings moved during the night. You wouldn't actually come in contact with the ghost, but you would notice that something had moved your stuff.

Beyond the custodial staff, no one is in the building late at night. While the custodians will report children's voices throughout the school, there is no one else who goes into the building late at night to confirm this experience. It seems to me that the only way to directly experience these ghosts would be to get a job as an overnight janitor at Anderson High School.

GRACE E. HUNT SCHOOL

Compton Road and Harrison Avenue, Cincinnati, OH 45231

directions

Take I-75 north to I-275 west. Take the Hamilton Avenue/US-127 exit off I-275. From the highway, head south toward Mt. Healthy. Take Hamilton Avenue to Compton Road and turn right. One block farther, you will see the school on the corner of Compton Road and Harrison Avenue.

history

This school was built in the 1860s as a small four-room building. It was expanded to an eight-room high school in 1893. The building that stands at the location today was built in 1910 and was named after schoolteacher Grace E. Hunt. She was the wife of one of the leaders of the Mt. Healthy educational system named Charles Hunt. She taught within the Mt. Healthy school system for forty years.

ghost story

The most widely reported ghost often will play with the lights on the third floor of the building. People walking or driving by late at night while the building is empty will see the lights on the third floor begin to flicker on and off repeatedly. Whenever those witnessing this phenomenon are able to check to make sure that the building is secure, the doors are always locked, and the building is empty.

Another, perhaps creepier, ghost activity also occurs here. Sometimes teachers will complete their lessons for the day and go home, and when they return the next morning, there are strange messages written on the chalkboard. Most of the time, these writings on the board are nothing more than scribbles that the teacher is sure weren't there when he or she left the room the day before, but other times, there are clear messages written on the boards—such as "Help me," or "Get out." Sometimes the messages will be complete lesson plans for a class that hadn't occurred in the room. Perhaps the ghosts who had occupied the room during the night had forgotten to erase the board after they had completed their nightly lessons.

visiting

Unfortunately, it is next to impossible to gain access to the inside of this building. It is currently a private school that doesn't like to speak about the reputed ghosts on the property. Even reputable authors or ghosthunting groups have been denied access. It seems the only way to get inside is to have a child who attends the school or to get a job at the school. If you try the latter approach, I wouldn't mention the fact that you are trying to investigate the paranormal activity.

In my opinion, the best way to visit this site is to watch the building at night from the outside and see if there are any lights flashing on the third floor.

MIAMITOWN ELEMENTARY SCHOOL
6578 State Route 128, Cleves, OH 45041

directions
Take I-75 north to I-74 to exit 7 (Hamilton/Cleves/128). Turn right (north) off the exit toward the gas stations and Wendy's. Across from the Miamitown Cemetery, you will see the elementary school. Turn right onto Mill Street to access the school's parking lot.

history
The site where the elementary school and its parking lot now sit was once the Municipal Cemetery in Miamitown. When it came time to build the school (originally it was Miamitown High School), officials wanted to locate the building on SR128 near the heart of town. Unfortunately, there was no room for it among the buildings already standing there. Officials felt it would be easier to move the Municipal Cemetery across the street to the churchyard to make way for the school rather than to destroy any of the existing buildings.

Workers meticulously moved the cemetery across the street, moving each headstone and body to another burial site in the churchyard. When all of the headstones were gone, they assumed that the work was done, but when they broke ground for the school and for the school's parking lot, they started digging up bodies. They dug up piles and piles of bodies. Apparently, many of the headstones in the original cemetery had become lost over time, so engineers were stuck with bodies whose identities had been completely lost. Unable to find out who these people were, they simply reburied the bodies in the churchyard without ceremony or markers.

ghost story

Many ghosts are said to roam the parking lot and elementary school at all hours of the day. At night, people report seeing shadowy figures roaming the parking lot, but the figures vanish when approached. These figures are especially prevalent on the east side of the lot near a line of trees and a tool shed. Other people walking through the lot will report being touched by some unseen hand on the back of their neck or on their arm. Still others will see figures walking around within the school building after hours, when the building is supposedly empty.

The most famous ghost of the school is a woman wearing a gray, nineteenth-century dress. She supposedly haunts a supply closet in the downstairs of the building. Teachers will often see her in this supply closet and will get a menacing vibe from her. Some teachers even refuse to enter the closet for fear that they will encounter this sinister apparition.

visiting

Unless you are a student or employee of the Miamitown Elementary School, you cannot enter the school building, making it next to impossible for to see the Lady in Gray. But you can always walk into the parking lot at night in an attempt to experience the ghosts there. Keep your eyes trained on the shed near the back of the lot or in the empty windows of the school building itself for your best chance of seeing something paranormal.

MOTHER OF MERCY HIGH SCHOOL
3036 Werk Road, Cincinnati, OH 45211

directions
Take I-74 west from Cincinnati to the Montana Avenue exit (exit 17). Turn left onto Montana and follow it up the hill until you get to Boudinot Avenue near the YMCA. Take a left on Boudinot. Follow Boudinot until you get to Werk Road, and then turn left on Werk Road. Mother of Mercy High School will be on your left.

history
This school was built in 1915 exclusively for girls in grades one through twelve. Most of the remainder of the building that stands today was finished by 1923. It continued to cater to girls of all ages until the late 1970s when it became strictly a high school.

The auditorium in the school is named after one of the nuns who taught there for most of her career—Sister Mary Carlos.

ghost story
The ghost of Mercy High School is that of Sister Mary Carlos—at least according to most of the students who work in the theater department who have experienced

this haunting. The students perform a ritual to appease the spirit that haunts the auditorium. Before the opening of a show, the director of the performance will go into the theater when no one else is there and light candles. She will then proceed to invite Sister Mary Carlos to the show. According to legend, if the students skip this ritual, Sister Mary Carlos will play havoc with the show on opening night.

There will be a variety of technical difficulties. The lights will flicker on and off for no reason, or the radio equipment will only carry static. Other times, props for the performance will be moved around, making it impossible to go on to the next scene without first finding where the props had been moved.

visiting

It is nearly impossible to enter the school with the sole intention of hunting for the ghosts. This particular haunting, however, offers people from outside the school the unique ability to enter the haunted auditorium. If the school is having a play, you can buy tickets and attend the opening night performance, when, if the ghost ritual is not performed, you might see a lot of technical problems caused by the feisty nun. If you want to see the ghost in action, opening night of a play at Mercy High School is your best bet.

MOUNT NOTRE DAME HIGH SCHOOL

711 East Columbia Avenue, Cincinnati, OH 45215

directions

Take I-75 north to Ronald Reagan Highway east to the Ridge Road exit. Turn north onto Ridge Road (left if you're headed east on Ronald Reagan, right if you're headed west on Ronald Reagan). Ridge Road will angle slightly to the left and change its name to East Columbia Avenue. The high school will be less than a half-mile down the road on the left.

history

One of the older schools in Cincinnati, this building opened in September of 1860 as a boarding school for girls. Two of General William T. Sherman's daughters went to this school in its early years. The school went through many changes through the years, even allowing male students at one point. At another point it included grades K–12. By 1956, it was the all-girl high school that it is today.

The darkest piece of the building's history occurred in the early 1940s, when a young female student killed herself here. She committed suicide on the third floor.

ghost story

All the ghostly activity in this building seems to be confined to the third floor. It is assumed that the ghost here is the young girl who committed suicide. Most of the time, the activity involves one of two things. The first one occurs when students come to class in the morning. They discover that all the lockers on the third floor have somehow opened up by themselves. The second thing that happens is that all the lights on the third floor will somehow turn on by themselves during the night. Even though the lights had been turned off and the lockers closed before the last person left for the night, people arrive the next morning to find the lights on and the lockers open.

visiting

The biggest problem with visiting this ghost is that all of the reported activity happens when no one is around. The lights will turn on, and the lockers will open when no one is in the building, which makes seeing this ghost next to impossible.

Your best bet to see ghostly activity in action is to go to the building late at night and watch the windows on the third floor. Perhaps those lights will come on as you watch. If they are already on, know that they are always turned off before the last person leaves for the day.

NORWOOD MIDDLE SCHOOL

2060 Sherman Avenue, Norwood, OH 45212

directions

Take I-75 north to the Norwood Lateral, exit 7. Take the US-22/Norwood/Montgomery Road exit off the lateral and then turn left onto Wesley Avenue. Take the first left onto Norwood Avenue. Turn left onto Montgomery Road. Then turn right onto Sherman Avenue. The middle school will be on your right.

history

Norwood Middle School was built in 1914 and originally served as Norwood's high school building. It continued to be the high school until 1972, when it became the middle school for seventh and eighth graders.

While the ghost story here involves a murder victim in the school, there is no historic record of any such murder happening within the building since its construction. If there is indeed the ghost of a murder victim who haunts the students, perhaps the victim was killed nearby or on the land where the school was built.

ghost story

A couple of ghosts have been frequently reported here at the Norwood Middle School. The first one is a ghost who haunts the school's auditorium. There is a balcony in the auditorium, and after certain performances and practices, people will hear clapping coming from the balcony. When they look up, they see a white glowing figure standing up and clapping.

The other ghost here doesn't seem to be nearly as supportive of the students and their efforts. This one is reputedly the ghost of a murder victim who was killed in the area. This ghost will be seen walking down the hallways of the school, bleeding from the wound that killed her in life. Sometimes, this ghost will even call out the name of the student who witnesses the phenomenon, scaring that child even more. The bleeding apparition will vanish into thin air almost as quickly as it appears.

visiting

Like many of the schools in this book, the ghosts here are quite difficult to visit if you're not a student or employee of the school. Schools do not cherish reputations for ghosts and spirits—for good reason. It's hard enough to get students to want to come to school in the first place. They don't want the students to be scared to come to school. For this reason it is essentially impossible to go to the school and investigate for paranormal phenomena.

This being said, one of the ghosts haunts the auditorium, and if you are interested in witnessing this ghost, you could buy a ticket and attend a student show. Make sure you look up to the balcony after the show when the applause begins.

OAK HILLS HIGH SCHOOL

3200 Ebenezer Road, Cincinnati, OH 45248

directions

Take I-75 north to I-74 west to the Harrison/Rybolt exit and follow Harrison Avenue up the hill until you see the Rave Cinemas on your left. At this point, turn right onto Filview Circle. Turn right again on Hutchinson Road and follow this road to the first traffic light. At this five-way traffic light, go straight. Hutchinson changes its name at this point to Ebenezer Road. Follow Ebenezer for about a mile. Oak Hills High School will be on your left.

history

There is not much history to tell about this building. There are no reports of anyone dying here. The school, which recently celebrated its fiftieth anniversary, is rather new compared to many of the public schools in the Cincinnati area. I'm not sure where the ghost came from, but there does seem to be something that haunts this building's stage.

ghost story

The theater at Oak Hills is supposedly haunted by a short old woman. The ghost here doesn't have a name, and no one really knows her origins. People who are in the theater before a performance will often see her on the stage looking around. They will approach her, and she will either disappear before their eyes, or they will chase her backstage only to find no sign of her.

Other things happen in the theater when the short old woman isn't around. The lights will flicker on and off for no reason. Strange sounds will echo through the theater from no known source. Sometimes the doors will slam closed and swing open for no reason. All of the ghostly activity in the building seems to be focused in the theater area.

visiting

Fortunately for those who work in the theater department, this ghost never seems to interrupt any performances. Unfortunately for us ghost enthusiasts, her lack of activity during the shows makes it difficult for us to see her. Like most high schools, in order to gain access you need to either attend the school or be employed by the school. Usually, though, when the school's theater is haunted, outsiders can pay to attend one of the shows in order to see their ghosts. Since this ghost doesn't appear during performances, she's very difficult to see.

If you do happen to attend one of the plays here at the high school, and if nothing strange happens before or after the performance, you can always scan the audience for a short old woman who is just sitting back and enjoying the show.

PEABODY HALL AND THE MARCUM CONFERENCE CENTER AT MIAMI UNIVERSITY

Western Drive, Oxford, OH 45056

351 North Fisher Drive, Oxford, OH 45056

directions

Take I-75 north from Cincinnati to I-275. Take I-275 west to exit 33, the Colerain Avenue/US-27 exit. Take US-27 north to Oxford to the campus of Miami University. (You will have to turn left in Millville to continue to follow US-27.) When you reach Miami University, turn right onto Western Drive just before you get to Bachelor Hall. Peabody Hall will be past the chapel on the left side. It is a large gray building. To get to the Marcum Conference Center, take the second right after Western Drive onto East High Street. Turn left onto Fisher Drive, and the building will be on your right.

history

In 1853, Peabody Hall was built as the original site of the Western Female Seminary and was named for its principal, Helen Peabody, who strongly opposed co-education. The building was originally used for dormitories for the Western Female Seminary and therefore exclusively housed women. In Room 210, a girl hung herself in one of the early years of the building's existence. Many years later, after the building became a co-ed dorm, another girl hung herself in the same room.

In 1856, Fisher Hall originally housed another female college, which was located on the outskirts of Miami University's campus. The female college eventually moved to a different building, and Fisher Hall became an asylum for the insane. While some of the stories from Fisher Hall date back to the time when the building was an asylum, the most famous ghost of the building is that of a student. On April 19, 1953, a young man returned to his room in Peabody Hall to find the door wide open and a textbook sitting out as though his roommate had been reading it. But the roommate was gone. The student assumed that his roommate, Ronald Tammen, had simply gone out for a walk and forgotten to close the door and put away his book. But Ronald Tammen never came back. In fact, he was never seen again. Fisher Hall was demolished in 1973 and the Marcum Conference Center was built on the site.

ghost story

The ghost stories involving Peabody Hall are usually attributed to either the ghost of Helen Peabody or to the ghosts of the girls who hung themselves in Room 210. Since Helen Peabody was very much against co-education, her ghost began haunting the building as soon as it became a co-ed dorm. People have seen her walking the hallways. Men who stand near the windows in the rooms are pushed toward the windows by some unseen force. Women who are sick in bed who attempt to get up for any reason are gently pushed back down. In the rooms, especially in Room 210, things will move around by themselves, and the blinds on the windows will flap violently despite the lack of a breeze.

Ronald Tammen is seen around campus and around the Marcum Conference Center. People describe him as wearing 1950s attire and as having some sort of injury to his head. These descriptions started rumors that the young man had been hit in the head and as a result had developed amnesia. Despite a massive search by both the university and the police after he was reported missing, he was never found. People continue to see him around campus and always describe him the same way, most often near the site of Fisher Hall—the place where he was last seen.

visiting

Peabody Hall sits in the Western College section of Miami University—one of the more beautiful areas on the campus, but it can be one of the creepier places to visit at night. Today it is the headquarters of the Western College program and holds dorms, offices, and a theater. Unfortunately, the building is difficult to access if you are searching for ghosts. If you are not a student or employee at the college, your best bet of encountering a ghost is probably going to be in the area surrounding the building. This area is wooded and rather creepy at night. Students often walk through the grounds to and from their dorms late at night, so if you were to explore the landscape near Peabody Hall long after dark, you would not even look out of place.

Marcum Conference Center is located near the Western Campus, and Ronald Tammen is sometimes seen near Peabody Hall as well as the area near the conference center. Most often, Ronald's ghost is seen in the remote wooded areas of campus. Look for a young man walking around with a dazed look on his face and with blood running from a cut on his forehead.

RAPID RUN MIDDLE SCHOOL

6345 Rapid Run Road, Cincinnati, OH 45233

directions

Take I-75 north to the Harrison Avenue exit. Follow the signs toward Queen City Avenue and follow Queen City up the hill until you get to the light at Sunset Avenue. Turn left on Sunset Avenue. The road will soon change its name to Rapid Run. Continue to follow Rapid Run for a few miles. The school will be on your left.

history

This school accommodates students from the fifth to the eighth grade. The piece of history that is most relevant to the ghost that supposedly haunts the building occurred during the construction of the auditorium in 2000. A worker who was standing on a tall ladder suddenly slipped and fell to the concrete floor below. The fall killed him instantly.

ghost story

Ghostly activity happens most often in the auditorium of this school. For no reason whatsoever, the lights inside of the auditorium will flash on and off during the day and at night. Chairs suddenly fall over and move. Other times, chairs will disappear and will later be found hidden in strange places throughout the building. People say that all of this is due to the ghost of the worker who was killed during the construction of the auditorium.

The playground at the small park behind the school is also reputed to be haunted. People will see ghostly children roaming through the playground at night. Children's voices and laughter can sometimes be heard from the playground, even when it's empty.

visiting

It is difficult but not impossible to gain access to the auditorium to witness the ghostly activity. Since this is a school, you are not allowed to enter the auditorium with the sole intention of looking for ghosts. You can, however, attend events staged in the auditorium, such as the school's annual musical, so if you are really interested in experiencing the ghost of the auditorium and you are not a student or employee, this is your best bet.

It is a little easier to witness the ghosts at the playground. The playground is outside and officially not a part of the school property, so you can go there in hopes of seeing the ghosts. Unfortunately, the playground is closed after dark. If you want to find the ghost, I would suggest going after school has let out for the day but before dark. This is when most of the activity is reported anyway.

OLD REILY HIGH SCHOOL

6093 Reily Millville Road, Oxford, OH 45056

directions

Take I-75 north to I-275 west. Take I-275 to the Colerain Avenue/US-27 exit and take US-27 north. Follow this road for about ten and a half miles past Ross until you are almost to the traffic light in Millville. Turn left onto OH-129/High Street. Follow OH-129 for about six miles and then turn right onto Sample Road/OH-732. Follow this road for about three miles into Reily. On your right, as Sample Road is coming to an end, you will be able to see the high school and the playground. If you turn right at the end of Sample Road at Main Street and then turn right again at Reily Pizza onto Reily Millville Road, you will come across the front of the old high school.

history

The building today is a community center, but originally, it was the high school for Reily Township. Perhaps the darkest piece of history of the school—and perhaps the reason for the ghostly occurrences—occurred in the 1950s. A student at the school had been dumped by his girlfriend, and unwilling to live the rest of his life without her, the young man walked back behind the west wing near where the small playground is today carrying a shotgun. He put the barrel in his mouth and shot himself to death there on school grounds.

ghost story

Reily is creepy at night, perhaps the creepiest little town I have ever visited in all my local ghosthunting adventures. The old school building looks abandoned, but it is, in fact, a community center. At night, the center is empty but often the lights will flash on and off for no reason.

The small playground behind the community center is also reputed to be haunted. People will hear sounds coming from there late at night when no one is around. The sounds of sobbing often are heard, but more often people will hear what sounds like a gunshot. When they investigate, they find no one nearby and see no damage that may have resulted from a gunshot.

Also, people often report a feeling of discomfort on the road just outside of the school leading down to Reily Pizza. People say they get chills down their spines and feel that some evil force is watching them when they are within that area late at night.

visiting

Reily is a very creepy place, especially late at night. I get the sense from many of the locals that they don't like people going through their town at that time. This feeling of unwelcome does add to the creepiness of the place. You do not want to walk into the playground at the old high school late at night because you will be considered a trespasser. Luckily, the school and playground are very near some main roads, and you easily can stand on the road and hear any sounds coming from the playground or see any lights flickering within the community center. If I were to hear a gunshot, though, I would jump in my car and leave rather than stay to investigate. The sound could come from a ghost, but I wouldn't want to stick around to find out for sure.

ST. XAVIER HIGH SCHOOL

600 West North Bend Road, Cincinnati, OH 45224

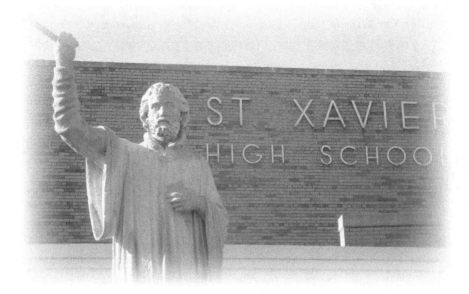

directions

Take I-75 north from downtown Cincinnati to I-275 west. Take I-275 to the Winton Road exit by the Cincinnati Mills Mall. Take Winton Road south for several miles until you get to North Bend Road. Turn left onto North Bend Road. Almost immediately after the turn from Winton Road, the road forks. Follow the left road in the fork to stay on North Bend. St. Xavier High School will be on your left.

history

St. Xavier High School is the oldest high school in Cincinnati. It hasn't always been in the same building, however. For most of its existence, it stood downtown near the corner of Seventh Street and Sycamore. In the 1950s the school moved to Finneytown and has been there ever since.

According to legend, there was a janitor who worked at the high school who was rather depressed. One day, he hung himself in a stall in the men's restroom on the first floor of the building.

ghost story

The ghost of the janitor is seen often throughout the halls of St. X High School. People will see a janitor who they don't recognize. That janitor will vanish suddenly right before their eyes. This apparition also is seen in the bathroom in which the janitor supposedly hung himself. People will see the janitor working in one of the stalls through a mirror in the bathroom, but when they turn around away from the mirror, the janitor has mysteriously vanished.

visiting

As is the case with most schools, it is difficult to test this ghost story for yourself unless you go to St. X High School or you work there. Understandably, the school is not receptive to ghost groups asking if they can come into the building to look for ghosts, so this building could prove to be almost impossible to enter with the intention of ghosthunting.

TAYLOR HIGH SCHOOL
36 Harrison Avenue, North Bend, OH 45052

directions

From Cincinnati, take Route 50 west all the way to the town of North Bend. Turn onto Miami Avenue by the sign pointing you to William Henry Harrison's tomb. Follow Miami Avenue up the hill to East Harrison Avenue. Turn right. The high school will be on your left.

history

This high school was founded in 1926 in the small town of North Bend, Ohio. The history behind the ghosts that reside here seems to focus on one incident—the tragic death of a custodian who worked at the school during the 1960s and 1970s. One night, this custodian was working alone in the building. Everyone else had left, and he had climbed a ladder to work on something near the ceiling. He suffered a heart attack while he was on the ladder, and he fell to the floor, unconscious. Since there was no one else in the building to help him, he died there on the floor at the foot of the ladder. He was found the next morning by a secretary who had arrived early. Not much is known about this custodian except that he liked to smoke cigars.

Another story about the school involves a student who had been talking on a cell phone and had managed to trip and fall into the swimming pool. He was wearing heavy clothing and was dragged to the bottom. By the time he was found, he had already drowned.

ghost story

One of the ghosts of the school seems to be that of the janitor who died here. People will sometimes report that they smell cigar smoke even though no one has been permitted to smoke a cigar in the building for ages. Since the custodian who died liked to smoke cigars, many people say that this is the ghost of the custodian. Other times, despite the fact that custodians swear that they closed all of the doors after cleaning the rooms, the doors to all of the classrooms will mysteriously open by themselves during the night.

Another ghost at the school seems to be that of the boy who drowned in the pool. The toilets in the locker room near the pool will flush by themselves, and people will hear frantic splashing coming from the pool and upon investigation find that the pool is empty.

visiting

Like many high schools, Taylor is quite hard to visit if you want to search for ghosts. You pretty much need to be a student or an employee here.

WESTERN HILLS HIGH SCHOOL

2144 Ferguson Road, Cincinnati, OH 45238

directions

Take I-75 north to the Harrison Avenue exit. Follow the signs to get to Queen City Avenue and follow Queen City up the hill until you get to Ferguson Road. Turn left onto Ferguson. Just past the Walmart, West High will be on your left.

history

This is one of the older public high schools in the city of Cincinnati. It has seen such famous graduates as Andy Williams and Pete Rose, and it was featured in the 1993 movie *Airborne*. It seems that very little tragedy has occurred at the school, which, while good for the school, makes it hard to rationalize the ghostly activity that happens here.

ghost story

The ghost story at this school is rather strange. Paranormal activity seems to happen mostly around the swimming pool area, and yet there doesn't seem to be any historical events to account for the ghost. One story goes that there was a foreign exchange student who had cut class and walked down to the swimming pool area to talk on his cell phone, and he fell in the water. He frantically splashed and called for help, and a custodian rushed to his aid. The custodian reported that it appeared that the student was being drug underneath the water by some unseen force. The student was saved and tragedy was averted, but no reason was found for why the student was being pulled under the water so forcefully. According to legend, the student fell into the pool at exactly 1:24 in the afternoon.

Many strange things will occur to this day by the swimming pool area. Most of the time these things will happen at exactly 1:24. People will hear frantic splashing coming from the pool or will hear screams. What makes these occurrences even stranger is that the pool is no longer in use and therefore no longer filled with water.

visiting

It is very difficult to visit the site of this haunting unless you are employed by the school or enrolled as a student. The building is off limits to visitors, especially areas such as the old swimming pool, which is off limits even to students. Nevertheless, for students and employees it is still possible to hear the ghostly splashing and screaming coming from the old pool. The facet of this haunting that makes it at least a little easier to encounter this ghost is that the phenomena always seem to happen at exactly the same time of day—1:24 in the afternoon while the students are still in class. Since you know what time the haunting takes place, it isn't difficult to be there when it happens.

CINCINNATI JOB CORPS

1409 Western Avenue, Cincinnati, OH 45214

directions

From downtown Cincinnati, take I-75 north to the Ezzard Charles Drive exit. Turn left onto Ezzard Charles toward the Museum Center and away from Music Hall. Ezzard Charles Drive dead-ends into the Museum Center. To the right of the Museum Center stands the Job Corps building. You can either pay to park at the Museum Center's lot and walk across the street to the Job Corps, or, since the road there is one way, you can turn left at the Museum Center and circle around to the Job Corps building and park on the street.

history

This building has a long history, many facets of which could have caused the hauntings that occur. At one point, the building was a convent, and many nuns lived here. According to legend, a nun once hung herself within these walls.

At another point, it was an armory, and at still another time it was a hospital. Beyond the nun who killed herself in the building, many witnesses suggest that the ghostly activity can be traced back to the time when it was a hospital. Many people died here during those years, many in traumatic and painful ways.

Today, the building houses the Cincinnati Job Corps school and dorms, and students report run-ins with the spirits who still haunt the halls.

ghost story

Many ghosts supposedly haunt this large building. The students who stay in the dorms here will often hear footsteps and voices coming from the hallway outside their rooms. When they open the door to see who is out there, the hallway is empty. Other times, strange things happen in the bathrooms throughout the building. People inside the stalls will hear someone walk in and flush a toilet, and will look underneath the stall only to see that there are no feet there. The restroom is empty. Other times, all the sinks in the restroom will turn on by themselves.

The most frequently sighted apparition is the ghost of the nun who killed herself while the building was a convent. She will be seen roaming the hallways, and other times students will report being shushed by an unseen voice.

Shadowy figures will sometimes chase people up the stairways at night, and all other kinds of dark apparitions will be seen throughout the building.

visiting

This is definitely one of the most difficult locations in the book to visit with the intention of looking for ghosts. The building is a boarding school, and the only people who have access to the areas where the ghosts are seen most often are the students and employees. Administration at the school will not be receptive if you ask to roam the halls looking for ghosts. In my opinion, the only way to search for the ghosts here is

to either work at or attend school here. Since the building is so close to other haunted places in the city, such as the Cincinnati Museum Center and Music Hall, it is definitely worth stopping by. Perhaps if you stop to admire the building from the outside, you will look up into one of the windows and see a nun looking back at you.

HOOVEN FIREHOUSE

311 Ohio Avenue, Hooven, OH 45033

directions

Take I-74 to exit 7, Cleves/Hamilton SR-128. Take 128 south several miles until you near the Kroger at the bottom of the road. Hooven sits on the hill behind the Kroger. Turn onto Childlaw Avenue off 128 to get into Hooven. Turn right onto Ohio Avenue. The fire station will be on your left as you drive down Ohio Avenue.

history

While this may sound like a paranormal cliché, Hooven was built on top of an ancient Indian burial ground. This large hill that stands near the Ohio River was considered sacred by the Native Americans who lived here, and it was used to bury many Native Americans.

Most of the ghost stories concern a fire chief who worked for many years at the Hooven Firehouse. After so much time he became kind of a fixture at the building. Eventually, the chief passed away from heart failure within the building itself.

ghost story

Most of the ghost stories involve phantom footsteps. The employees often hear footsteps echoing through the building, but they will be unable to find the source of these footsteps. What makes this story more interesting is that the footsteps sound like they are made by a particular type of boot that only a couple of the firefighters wear—and the fire chief who passed away wore that type of boot.

One time the firefighters painted the floor of the garage, and they roped off the entire area. When they came back after the paint had dried, they found a footprint in the paint that had the tread from the same type of boot that the chief would wear. At the time of the painting, the only man still working at the fire station who wore that type of boot was out of town.

Other times, people will feel incredibly uncomfortable inside the building. Brave firefighters will wake up in the middle of the night after napping at the station and will feel that there is an ominous presence behind them.

visiting

This building is still an active station that is used as the firehouse in Hooven. It is not open to the public and is therefore difficult to enter to search for ghosts. The staff at the firehouse is very open about their ghosts, and if they aren't busy when you visit, you could ask them if you can look around for one of the ghosts that supposedly haunts the building. The worst they can do is say no.

MT. SAINT JOSEPH MOTHERHOUSE

Corner of Bender Road and Delhi Pike, Cincinnati, OH 45233

directions

From downtown Cincinnati, go west on Route 50 until you get to Bender Road. Turn right onto Bender Road and follow it until it dead ends. This huge building occupies the corner of Bender Road and Delhi Pike. It is on the campus of Mt. Saint Joseph College.

history

The Motherhouse was built by the Sisters of Mercy in the late 1800s. By 1884, the building was completed as a convent and living space for the nuns there. Unfortunately, that same year the building burned to the ground. Several nuns were caught in the building and perished in the fire.

The Motherhouse was the original location of Mt. Saint Joseph College, which was originally a school exclusively for girls. When it was rebuilt after the fire, it continued to be a convent used to house nuns who were affiliated with the Sisters of Mercy. A cemetery was created on the grounds of the Motherhouse, and this cemetery is still in use today.

ghost story

Many nuns have lived in this building, and many have died here. People will often see nuns walking the hallways of this vast building, and sometimes these nuns will be wearing the old style of habit, a uniform that isn't in use today but was in use during the time of the fire in 1884. When these nuns are approached, they either disappear, or they turn to reveal that they have been badly burned, with flesh hanging off their face and hands. These are most likely the spirits of the nuns who were killed in the fire. Other times people will see figures roaming the cemetery at night. These figures will vanish into thin air when they are approached.

visiting

This building is next to impossible to visit and is essentially impossible to investigate. Outsiders are not allowed to enter. It is not open to any kind of public tours or visits despite being such an historic building. Even students and employees at the College of Mount Saint Joseph are not permitted in the building. Only those nuns who belong to the order and their families are allowed in at any time. The nuns are not receptive to people who want to search for ghosts. The ghost stories travel quietly between the nuns or are seen by visitors during the day. The official stance by the Sisters of Mercy is that there are no ghosts in these halls. So if you were to ask them if you could stage a paranormal investigation in their building, you will definitely get a firm 'no.'

The only place to investigate is the cemetery, but this is also quite an undertaking. Only those who live and work in the Motherhouse and their families can park in the lot. The cemetery also closes at night, and you will be arrested if you are found there—the "searching for ghosts" excuse will not get you off the hook.

Your best bet is to simply admire the haunted historic building from afar and maybe roam the cemetery while it's open during the day. If I were you, though, I wouldn't break out the EMF detector while you're roaming through the cemetery. My guess is that you would be asked to leave.

SATAN'S HOLLOW

4150 Hunt Road, Cincinnati, OH 45236

directions

This location has been notoriously difficult to find for many curious ghosthunters, but it does exist. To get there, take I-75 north to Cross County Highway east to the Reed Hartman Highway exit. Turn left on Reed Hartman and follow it north until you get to Hunt Road. Turn left on Hunt and park behind the Kmart. You will walk past an apartment complex and into the woods located behind the Kmart. When you reach the woods, you will come across a small creek with a wooded hill behind it. Cross the creek and climb the hill. Beyond the hill you'll find another creek. Follow it upstream. At the end of this creek is a tunnel system, covered with graffiti and known to the locals and Cincinnati area ghosthunters as Satan's Hollow.

history

Why is there a tunnel out in the middle of the woods in Blue Ash? It was part of the old Blue Ash sewer system many years ago. This section of the sewage system eventually went out of service, and the tunnels were simply abandoned in the woods. Now the tunnels are part of a large system used to drain rainwater from the road down to the creek. Local teenagers and delinquents discovered this secluded tunnel and have since covered most of it with graffiti. Unfortunately, the rumors about the ghosts at the tunnel have increased the incidents of vandalism here.

ghosts

Ghost stories about this area are often quite dark, and they suggest that the ghosts are dangerous. The legend goes that a group of Satanists used the old abandoned sewer tunnels in the woods in Blue Ash for their ceremonies. There is even a room within the tunnels called the altar room where there is a block of stone that resembles an altar. Rumors exist that this was where the group actually summoned a demon, one that haunts these tunnels to this day.

People will feel extreme discomfort within the tunnels and will often feel physically sick. Dark figures will be seen lurking within the tunnels. Whenever these figures are investigated, no sign of anyone can be found. Voices and footsteps echo loudly throughout these tunnels, but sometimes voices will be heard even when no one is speaking. Other times people will see an ominous figure that approaches them aggressively in the darkness, sometimes actually scratching them and leaving physical marks on their skin.

visiting

Whether or not you believe the story of the evil demonic presence that haunts these tunnels, you should still exercise caution when approaching this haunted location. First of all, it's in a wooded area so if you visit it during the spring or summer, wear long pants and keep close watch for poison ivy and other natural hazards. Also, though the neighborhood is safe, there is extensive and profane graffiti throughout the tunnels, suggesting that some unsavory characters could be around. If you were to approach the tunnels, especially at night, and you were to see a figure deep within the tunnels, it may not be the dark demon that you were hoping to photograph.

There are no signs posted outside the tunnels about trespassing, but they are city property so you would probably be asked to leave if caught inside the tunnels. Also, the tunnels are abnormally dark so if you want to find the fabled 'altar room,' you will definitely need a flashlight.

CINCINNATI SUBWAY

Central Parkway between Hopple Street and the Western
Hills Viaduct, Cincinnati, OH 45225

directions

The most visible entrances to the Cincinnati Subway are along I-75. Two large metal
doors stand alongside the highway just north of the Western Hills Viaduct. If you take
the Western Hills Viaduct to Central Parkway and head north on Central Parkway, you
can park your car and get a better view of these entrances.

history

In 1920, the city of Cincinnati began work to install a subway system to aid those
people living in the outlying suburbs in their commute. By the time the Depression hit
in 1929, the subway was only partially complete. The city no longer had the funding
necessary to complete the project, so officials decided to cease construction.

For a while, the empty subway tunnels sat abandoned underneath the city,
but since they ran underneath working roads, officials had to make sure that the
tunnels remained stable to prevent a collapse. Because they were spending so much

money on the upkeep of the tunnels, city officials attempted to come up with uses for them.

During the Cold War, the tunnels were set up as shelters in case of nuclear attack. They were never used in this capacity, but to this day, there are remnants of these bomb shelters in the tunnels. Eventually, the city allowed the Cincinnati Water Works to run large water mains through the tunnels, and these are still there today. Unfortunately, these water mains make it very difficult to gain access to the tunnels. Officials do not allow just anyone to access the city's water in this manner.

ghost story

Most of the ghost stories from these tunnels are not very specific as to their historical truth. Stories say that many people died during the construction of the tunnels and these people continue to haunt the unfinished tracks. People will see shadowy figures walking through the tunnels when no one is there. People will hear voices and screams coming from within the tunnels when the tunnels are empty.

The most famous story about the tunnels is that, according to legend, the man who designed the tunnels became depressed when he found out that the subway would not be completed. He ended up walking into the tunnels one night and hanging himself. The ghost story goes that sometimes when you're walking through the tunnels at night, you will see the shadow of what looks like a man hanging by a noose. When you approach this hanging man, you discover that there is nothing there.

visiting

Unfortunately, this location is next to impossible to visit. The entrances to the tunnels are blocked by large metal doors. There is graffiti throughout the tunnels, suggesting that some people have found a way in, but most of the graffiti was done before the large metal doors were put in place.

This isn't to say that it's impossible to gain entrance to the subway system. The Cincinnati Museum Center used to take one tour a year through the subway. Last I heard, these tours cost sixty dollars and were booked up far in advance, so if you are interested in taking one of these tours, contact the Museum Center.

WESTWOOD TOWN HALL

3017 Harrison Avenue, Cincinnati, OH 45211

directions

Take I-75 north to I-74 west to the Montana Avenue exit. At the end of the ramp turn left to go up the hill. Montana Avenue will take you into the heart of Westwood. When you get to the intersection of Montana Avenue and Harrison Avenue, the Westwood Town Hall is the large building across Harrison on your right.

history

The Westwood Town Hall was built in 1889. At the time, Westwood was trying to become a large village on the outskirts of Cincinnati. Unfortunately, the lack of easy transportation to the village hurt its growth. In the mid-1870s, attempts were made to put a rail line through Westwood, but the funding fell through. By 1889, when the town hall was built, the town had only about one thousand residents.

The town hall housed most of the village government at the time. The seat of government and all elected offices met here. The building also housed the fire department of Westwood and the town jail.

During one point in the history of the building, a caretaker named Wesley worked and lived in the building. According to legend, he was a trustworthy security guard who was deeply devoted to the building itself. He lived in the area downstairs that is occupied by classrooms today. In 1896, when the town of Westwood was absorbed into the City of Cincinnati and his services were no longer needed at the building, he was fired. Unwilling to leave the building to which he had become so attached, he hung himself in the attic.

ghost story

There are many stories about ghosts here at the Westwood Town Hall. Many people say that these stories center on the ghost of Wesley, who they claim is a protective spirit. He will do anything to protect the building and those who visit it. No one ever seems to get hurt inside the building, which some attribute to the watchful eyes of Wesley.

Other times, Wesley seems to get a little more mischievous and angry. Things throughout the building get rearranged during the night despite no one having been inside the building. Doors and windows will open and slam shut for no reason. Others have actually seen a male figure who walks the halls and then mysteriously vanishes. Wesley is most often seen in the attic of the building, or from the outside in the bell tower that overlooks the street.

visiting

Westwood Town Hall isn't easy to visit, especially when your intent is to look for ghosts. The people who run the building are very familiar with Wesley, and many of them enjoy the fact that they have a ghost on the property, but so many meetings and events go on inside the building that the administration cannot let just anyone come in and search for ghosts.

There are a several organizations that operate inside the building, including the Cincinnati Recreation Commission, which holds classes here. These classes run throughout the day and are listed on the commission's Web site. Most of these classes cost fifteen dollars, and you are confined to your classroom, unable to wander around looking for the ghost of Wesley.

There are also theater performances presented at the town hall. These will cost money, of course, and you will be confined to the theater.

Your best bet to catch a glimpse of Wesley is to watch the bell tower from the street. Wesley is often seen on that balcony, and you are always allowed to stand and watch for him.

Entrance gate at Coney Island Amusement Park, see profile on pages 86-87.

APPENDIX I

CHAPTERS ORGANIZED GEOGRAPHICALLY

Hamilton County

West side:

Congress Green Cemetery

Taylor High School

Hooven Firehouse

Miamitown Cemetery

Miamitown Elementary

Harrison's Dead Man's Curve

Miamitown Bridge

East Miami River Road

Buffalo Ridge Road

Rave Cinemas Western Hills

Oak Hills High School

Smokin' Monkey

Dillard's at Western Woods Mall

Western Hills High School

Price Hill Potter's Field

Dunham Park

Adath Israel Cemetery

Rapid Run Park

Western Hills Country Club

Crow's Nest

Rapid Run Middle School

Mercy High School

Westwood Town Hall

Darby Lee Historic Cemetery

Mt. St. Joseph Motherhouse

Delhi Park

Sedamsville Woods

A REAL-LIFE GHOST HUNTER'S POINT OF VIEW

Ray Lykins—Co-Founder, Cincinnati Regional Association for Paranormal Studies (CRAPS)

THE STONELICK COVERED BRIDGE is one of many urban legends that dictates you must flash your headlights three times to see an apparition appear out of thin air. There are several other legends about this area. If you go down Baizhiser Lane, legend holds, you will be chased by cult members. There are creepy houses that supposedly reflect the exact number of lights equal to the occupants in your car. Down the road further there is a ruined building known as the Devils Church. While there were some things that we were unable to do in the area, we did have creepy experiences. It was almost as if we were being watched by a group of people in a car to the side of the road that seemed to come out of nowhere as we pulled up close to a haunted location on Baizhiser Lane. They sped away as we decided to turn back and not enter. The bridge, while beautifully creepy, never produced apparitions no matter how many times we flashed our lights.

Hamilton County (*continued*)

Colerain and Mt. Healthy area:
Lick Road
Buell Road
Grace E. Hunt School
Mt. Healthy Alleys
Mt. Healthy Museum
St. Xavier High School

Downtown area:
Cincinnati Art Museum
Cincinnati Job Corps
Cincinnati Museum Center
Cincinnati Subway
Music Hall
Omni Netherland Plaza
Taft Theater
Taft Museum
Eden Park
Wesleyan Cemetery
Spring Grove Cemetery
Vernon Manor Hotel
Omni Netherland Plaza
Taft Theater
Taft Museum
Eden Park
Art Museum
Wesleyan Cemetery
Spring Grove Cemetery
Vernon Manor Hotel
Cincinnati Zoo

Norwood area:
Norwood Library
Norwood Middle School
U.S. Playing Card Company
Mt. Notre Dame High School

East Side:
Skytop Bigg's
Walton Creek Theater
Coney Island
Anderson High School
Hyde Park Graeter's
20th Century Theater
Habit's Café
Promont House
Latitudes
Loveland Madeira Road
Spooky Hollow Bridge
Blome Road Bridge
Camp Dennison
Heritage Village
Satan's Hollow

Butler County

Millville and Reily area:
Highway to Heaven
Millville Cemetery
Reily Cemeteries
Reily High School
Reily Pizza

Oxford area:
Peabody Hall
Oxford Milford Road
Hopewell Cemetery

A REAL-LIFE GHOST HUNTER'S POINT OF VIEW

Matt Hoskins—Investigator, Cincinnati Paranormal

WHEN I WAS YOUNG, the family tradition was Easter lunch at the Golden Lamb. Not only was the food fantastic, but I always loved the atmosphere and history that came with it. One time, our waitress mentioned that the place was haunted. She told us about guests who woke up to find someone in their room, who would vanish seconds later. I remember being enthralled with the idea, and during every visit after that, I would wander around the rooms upstairs, secretly hoping to see a ghost. And although I never saw one, I think the Golden Lamb is largely responsible for my love of both history and the paranormal. I believe the two go together, for what are spirits if not ephemeral fragments of the past?

Hamilton:
Butler County Fairgrounds
Princeton Road
New London Road

Middletown:
Woodside Cemetery
Sorg Opera House

Fairfield and West Chester area:
Beth Israel Cemetery
Harbin Park
Fairfield Lanes
White House Inn
Screaming Bridge

Warren County

Mason area:
McClung House
Rose Hill Cemetery
Kings Island

Kings Island Cemetery
Peter's Cartridge Company

Lebanon area:
Golden Lamb
Glendower Mansion
Spook Hollow

Clermont County

Loveland Castle
Old Miamiville Train Tracks
Peaceful Valley
Pond Run Road
Clermont County Dead Man's Curve

Northern Kentucky

Southgate House
Bobby Mackey's Music World
Shimmers
Narrow's Road

APPENDIX II
DAYTRIPPING [or in this case, NIGHTTRIPPING]

THE PARANORMAL PUB CRAWL
The Best Spirits in Town!

1ST STOP Shimmers Ballroom and Tavern

2ND STOP Bobby Mackey's Music World

3RD STOP Southgate House

4TH STOP Crow's Nest

5TH STOP Smokin' Monkey

6TH STOP Habit's Café

FINAL STOP Latitudes

(Remember, do not drive drunk. The city has enough ghosts. We don't want you making more.)

A REAL-LIFE GHOST HUNTER'S POINT OF VIEW

Melinda Smith—Founder, Southern Ohio Apparition Researchers (SOAR)

SOAR HAS BEEN CONTACTED BY MANY of the locals around the area who told us of their experiences. In one story, a local fire department was responding to an accident here and was using a thermal camera to look for hotspots in a car. They panned to the front of the car and saw a human figure curled up on the ground. When they went to check the person, there was no one there. In another story, some of our clients were in their car and stopped at the intersection one night about 1:30 a.m. They suddenly saw a man come out of the tree line who started chasing their car. They said he looked like a tall shadowy man who moved with amazing speed. As they took off, they looked back and he was gone. Beware: this is an extremely dark and dangerous intersection! SOAR has had the opportunity to investigate the location on two separate occasions. Even the best night-vision cameras need additional light sources to capture images. We waited for the apparition and the ghost cars to show themselves, but we were not lucky those two nights. Maybe they knew what we were there for, or maybe they like to prey on people who are alone.

THE URBAN LEGEND TRIP

Are they just urban legends, or is there something more?

1ST STOP Hook Man of Pond Run Road

2ND STOP Flash your lights at Stonelick Covered Bridge

3RD STOP Flash your lights at Buell Road

4TH STOP Pick up a Phantom Hitchhiker at Princeton Road on your way to...

5TH STOP Flash your lights at Oxford Milford Road

DOWN HARRISON AVENUE

A long road with a frightful variety of ghosts

1ST STOP Start by swerving down the Harrison Avenue's Dead Man's Curve

2ND STOP then cross the Miamitown Bridge

3RD STOP catch a scary movie at Rave Cinemas Western Hills

4TH STOP then stop at the Smokin' Monkey for a night cap

5TH STOP before saying good night to Wesley at the Westwood Town Hall

THE DEMONS OF SOUTHWEST OHIO

If you don't mess with them, they're still going to mess with you

1ST STOP Buffalo Ridge Road—have the Satanists in the woods gone too far?

2ND STOP Reily Cemetery—where the evil is almost tangible

3RD STOP Reily Pizza—the center of the pentagram

4TH STOP Satan's Hollow—where a demon protects the satanic altar

SEE HOW MANY HITCHHIKERS YOU CAN PICK UP

Those roadside phantoms with somewhere to be

1ST STOP Harrison Avenue's Dead Man's Curve—go ahead, pick him up if you have the guts.

2ND STOP East Miami River Road—the headless woman in the wedding dress is looking for something so why not give her a hand?

3RD STOP New London Road—all that jogging has to be tiring so give him a ride.

4TH STOP Princeton Road—hurry, she's running late for the prom!

5TH STOP Pond Run Road—the hook man would put out his thumb, if he had one.

6TH STOP Clermont Dead Man's Curve—if he doesn't have a face, how can he tell you where he wants to go?

GHOSTS OF THE CIVIL WAR

Who knew that the war was still going on?

1ST STOP Congress Green Cemetery—Union Soldiers walk among the fallen

2ND STOP Miamitown Bridge—a replacement for the one destroyed by General Burnside

3RD STOP Old Miamiville Train Tracks—General Morgan's civilian victim

4TH STOP Camp Dennison—the beginning and the end for many Union soldiers

5TH STOP Peter's Cartridge Company—munitions providers for the Union cause

APPENDIX III

PARANORMAL INVESTIGATION GROUPS

Got Ghosts?

You're not alone. Here is a list of some of the paranormal investigation groups from the Cincinnati area.

Cincinnati Paranormal

The focus of Cincinnati Paranormal is to come up with and utilize new ideas in the hopes of both helping out our clients and pushing forward the paranormal field as a whole. Our six members have over thirty years of experience in the paranormal field, giving us the unique opportunity to set up a group where everyone has the same say in the direction the group is taking. This offers the opportunity for many new ideas and strategies that the group and the paranormal field as a whole can take.

We are a non-profit group who will not charge you for an investigation of your home. It is our goal to help out people who are being haunted, so if something is happening in your house that you simply do not understand, please look us up on the web at www.cincinnatiparanormal.com or give us a call at (513) 407-4242.

A REAL-LIFE GHOST HUNTER'S POINT OF VIEW

Rick Fenbers—Co-Founder, The Cincinnati Regional Association for Paranormal Studies (CRAPS)

SATAN'S HOLLOW IS AN URBAN LEGEND that is known by many but experienced by very few. Deep, dark, and very creepy, its entrance hidden down in the woods, it's unlike any other location in the area. Looking into these tunnels, you have no way of knowing who, or what, is waiting for you inside. The day I found Satan's Hollow, as I stood at the entrance, I could see and hear "something" moving in the darkness inside. A fellow explorer? The Shadow man of the myth? Or my imagination run wild? I still don't know what it was. This is the one urban legend I've found that actually lives up to the hype surrounding it. Haunted or not, this is by far one of the creepiest locations in the Cincinnati area.

Northern Kentucky Paranormal Society (NKYPS)

We are a dedicated team in conducting paranormal research. We are very serious about our investigations which we perform as a service to the community and always place the safety and well being of our client and of our team above all else. NKYPS will always do our utmost to authenticate phenomena through the use of scientific equipment. Emotional support is also of utmost importance when working with individuals who find themselves in this situation—this applies whether our team has any findings or not. Each person's experience is valid for them

If the need of the client is beyond our scope or ability, we will make every effort to locate an individual who has the proper knowledge to offer assistance. We do not charge for our services. Our team considers it a privilege to be allowed into someone's home or business and entrusted with this sensitive problem. Our investigations will remain confidential and no information will ever be shared unless permission is given by the client.

Our team is comprised of individuals of many abilities including those whose specialties include electronics, EVP analysis, and historical research. We all have personal reasons for researching in this field that mostly stem from personal experiences and fascination with this subject. Whatever our reasons, we all possess a passion for this work.

Tri-State Paranormal of Northern Kentucky

My name is Chris Maggard, and I started researching in the paranormal field in my early teens. After moving to Northern Kentucky in 2004, I continued my research and investigations. Co-Founders Marybeth Stagman and Tracy Wilson helped me form Tri-State Paranormal of Northern Kentucky in 2009. We truly believe in ghosts/spirits and continue to develop new tools and techniques to advance our research and help our clients. Our clients' respect and wishes are held in high regards; their fears and concerns are never ignored.

Southern Ohio Apparition Researchers

The paranormal group Southern Ohio Apparition Researchers (SOAR) is located about twenty minutes east of Cincinnati in historically haunted New Richmond, Ohio. SOAR was founded in 2005 by Melinda Smith and has investigated over sixty locations since that time, covering Ohio, Kentucky, and Indiana. SOAR takes pride in helping their clients using scientific methods to find solutions to their paranormal troubles, and

A REAL-LIFE GHOST HUNTER'S POINT OF VIEW

Chris Maggard—Co-Founder, Tri State Paranormal of Northern Kentucky (TSP)

AFTER EXTENSIVE RESEARCH and two investigations, we have captured some truly interesting evidence about Skimmers. In the first investigation we captured what we believe is a full-bodied apparition walking across the main bar area. Also, in the basement there are several rooms with showers and lockers plus a few large rooms for what we now know was used for gaming and prostitution. While conducting our audio session in the basement, we captured EVPs in German and a woman sobbing. In the second investigation we captured more of a women's voice moaning, a man whispering the word "whiskey," and video footage of a dollar lifting up. This is truly an interesting place to investigate.

continues to follow up until they feel comfortable in their home or business. SOAR consists of not only paranormal researchers but also historical researchers who strive to find out the history of any paranormal location.

Cincinnati Regional Association for Paranormal Studies

Looking for the stories behind the myths? Come to www.oh-craps.com, home of the Cincinnati Regional Association for Paranormal Studies, featuring the "Paranormal Road trip," where we tell you the truth behind all those urban legends from Cincinnati and beyond. Want C.R.A.P.S. for an investigation in your home, business, or to check out an urban legend? Contact us at help@oh-craps.com or by calling 513-442-0982.

Paranormal Researchers of Northern Kentucky

Paranormal Researchers of Northern Kentucky (P.R.O.N.K.) is a free service to every person who is in need of answers or has experiences they want to verify with what we call "Para Forensic Research." Our group is mainly targeted to what is "real" and what is just "unknown." Instead of following the standards from the field, we step it up a notch. All of our investigators are trained to disprove a haunting rather than to prove one is there. This relates to real "scientific research." For something to be

A REAL-LIFE GHOST HUNTER'S POINT OF VIEW

Joy Naylor—Investigator, Cincinnati Paranormal

I HAD THE PRIVILEGE TO INVESTIGATE the Glendower Mansion back in 1995. It was just before their opening for the candlelight holiday tours. After a tour of the property, I began to set up my equipment on the first floor. As I was setting up, I noticed a glowing light moving up the staircase. I assumed that it was the caretaker going upstairs. When I turned back toward what I was doing, the caretaker was standing in front of me. He had just seen what I saw. Eyes wide and heart pounding with camera and recorder in hand, we moved toward the staircase and ascended. We found nothing upstairs. Moving room to room in the darkness upstairs, I clearly heard the sounds of music downstairs. We moved back downstairs, and the music stopped. Checking all the rooms downstairs—nothing. We were alone. These types of events happened many times throughout the night, moving from downstairs to upstairs. I think the "ghosts" were having great fun with me that night and I with them. The only evidence that I collected from that investigation was a piece of audio, the sounds of a crackling fire. The experience was incredible and is etched in my memory banks forever.

proven, the null hypothesis has to be rejected. We make a null hypothesis based on the owners' claims and try to see what exactly can be dis-proven or explained. After that, we go over the evidence and present it to our clients in a fashion to which they can decide the meaning. This field is yet to be proven and is free for all to decide what exactly paranormal activity is. We just try to provide reasoning and solid evidence to what exactly is going on in your place of residence or business. Feel free to contact Mike Hon or Keleah Collins at (859) 802-4719 or Paratudies@gmail.com. Check out our website @ pronk.yolasite.com

Southern Ohio Paranormal Research

Established in 2005, Southern Ohio Paranormal Research is happy to provide free paranormal investigation services to those in need. With three regional teams in Ohio, we are able to focus our attention on our clients. Our founder, James Bell, formed Southern Ohio Paranormal Research in the hopes of finding the answers people were looking for.

While we are still asking questions ourselves, we want to make it clear we will treat you and your situation with professionalism and care. We understand you may be confused about who to turn to, and Southern Ohio Paranormal Research will answer any questions you may have. To get in touch with us, just go to our website at http://southernohioparanormal.org/; if you are in need of an investigation please click on the Request Help link.

We hope you find the answers you are looking for and feel free to join our forums to participate in the ongoing discussions.

Tristate Paranormal and Oddities Observation Practitioners (TriPOOP)

Tristate Paranormal and Oddities Observation Practitioners is a group based out of the Tristate area (Ohio, Indiana, Kentucky). As our name suggests, we are committed to observing paranormal and odd occurrences. Using equipment such as digital voice recorders, digital cameras, full-spectrum film cameras, EMF and temperature meters, we try to figure out what we are observing to the best of our abilities. If you have a paranormal or odd occurrence and would like to have it investigated, look us up on the web. With our constantly growing member base, TriPOOP is always ready for an investigation.

A REAL-LIFE GHOST HUNTER'S POINT OF VIEW

Noah Carlisle—Investigator, Cincinnati Paranormal

THIS WAS ONE OF THE FIRST PLACES I ever investigated, and I did so even before I was ever a ghost investigator. I remember driving to the site with some friends in the car. I flashed my headlights three times and sure enough, I saw the light. Not expecting this ghost story to be true, I was stunned. I took off driving toward it, but unfortunately, I lost sight of it. From then on, I was always interested in stories and legends like this one and in those stories still waiting to be discovered.

ABOUT THE AUTHORS

JEFF AND MICHAEL MORRIS have been heavily involved with the paranormal field since 2005, when they started writing their first book, *Haunted Cincinnati and Southwest Ohio*. At around the same time, they started a ghost tour in Miamitown, Ohio, called Miamitown Ghost Tours, where patrons can experience the haunted history of this small town in Southwestern Ohio. Jeff and Michael also host an online paranormal radio show called Miamitown Ghost Talk on ASPRN.com, on which they have the opportunity to speak with big names in the field and to just speak about ghosts in general.

They also do a lot of paranormal investigation themselves. While researching this book, they went out to all of these places in an attempt to find the spirits who reside there, and beyond these trips, they are members of Cincinnati Paranormal, a paranormal investigation group.

Jeff has his degree in English from the haunted Miami University in Oxford, Ohio. He lives in the Covedale suburb of Cincinnati with his wife and two children. Michael has a degree in graphic design and lives in Miamitown with his wife and their three children.

Printed in the USA
CPSIA information can be obtained
at www.ICGtesting.com
JSHW060927260124
55822JS00006B/15